Teaching Realistic Optimism

Teaching Realistic Optimism

How to Approach Teaching and Learning with Hope

Ginna Guiang-Myers

ROWMAN & LITTLEFIELD
Lanham • Boulder • New York • London

Published by Rowman & Littlefield
An imprint of The Rowman & Littlefield Publishing Group, Inc.
4501 Forbes Boulevard, Suite 200, Lanham, Maryland 20706
www.rowman.com

86-90 Paul Street, London EC2A 4NE

Copyright © 2023 by Ginna Guiang Myers

All rights reserved. No part of this book may be reproduced in any form or by any electronic or mechanical means, including information storage and retrieval systems, without written permission from the publisher, except by a reviewer who may quote passages in a review.

British Library Cataloguing in Publication Information Available

Library of Congress Cataloging-in-Publication Data

Names: Guiang Myers, Ginna, author.
Title: Teaching realistic optimism : how to approach teaching and learning with hope / Ginna Guiang Myers.
Description: Lanham, Maryland : Rowman & Littlefield, 2023. | Includes bibliographical references.
Identifiers: LCCN 2022043900 (print) | LCCN 2022043901 (ebook) | ISBN 9781475856835 (cloth) | ISBN 9781475856842 (paperback) | ISBN 9781475856859 (ebook)
Subjects: LCSH: Teaching—Psychological aspects. | Teachers—Psychology. | Teachers—Job satisfaction. | Optimism.
Classification: LCC LB1027 .G783 2023 (print) | LCC LB1027 (ebook) | DDC 371.102—dc23/eng/20221108
LC record available at https://lccn.loc.gov/2022043900
LC ebook record available at https://lccn.loc.gov/2022043901

Contents

Acknowledgments	vii
Introduction	1
1 Defining Optimism and the Optimism Continuum: Why Is It More Than Just Positive Thinking?	5
2 The Negativity Bias: Classroom Manifestations and Ways of Addressing	19
3 Realistic Optimism and Explanatory Styles	33
4 Cycle of Fear and Learned Helplessness	47
5 Realistic Optimism, Hope, Decompression, and Emotional Detachment	59
6 Humor as a Pathway to Hope	75
7 Check Your Attitude to Boost Job Satisfaction	87
References	109

Acknowledgments

There are so many people (and also inanimate objects) I am indebted to for the development of this book. I must confess that I have lost hope (is this not ironic?), several times, of ever finishing this book. I have doled out copious amounts of inappropriate words and hurled some objects (no one was hurt) while writing it, during the many times of frustrations I have experienced. This book was written during the pandemic. And it was written because of the pandemic. It is now 2022, and it seems that we are about to finish the pandemic as I finish this book.

I wish to express gratitude to my daughter, Anyssa, and my son, Jared. I do not know what I did to deserve such kids, and I still carry the guilt of not being even a good enough mother. I know I left you when you were both very young—but know that that remains the darkest point in my life—and I still wish I had made the correct decisions. I wish I could have a "redo and retake" of the past, but I choose to focus on the future. I love you both dearly, and this book is dedicated to both of you.

There were many people all throughout the years who taught me what hope and optimism means (and some who gave me important lessons by modeling *quite the opposite*), and I wish to acknowledge all of them, as they have all enriched my life and have given me hope:

1. Callie, Porscha, and Joey: All my dogs have taught me how to look at life from an optimistic lens! My dogs are happy regardless of what toy I give them. They are supposed to be the most vicious breed—all

are rescued pit bulls—but they are the most loving dogs! Now, how can we not do zoomies like they do?
2. Lisa Blake and Gina Willis: These teachers constitute a ray of sunshine for me! They possess a contagious, extraordinary zest for learning! And though by fate we sometimes sit at opposite sides of the district negotiations table, they have remained my friends and fierce advocates, and unpaid therapists many times. They also have a patio that allows for safe venting.
3. Joyce Childs: my very extroverted friend! We have our disagreements, but I know you will always have my back! Thank you for always being hopeful and cheerful.
4. Sue Taylor: Through you allowing me to vent and express my frustrations, you have been a solid rock! I still remember the first LCAP meeting you attended when you proclaimed to everyone that *they* (the district) should "keep me"! I was at my lowest point at that time (my first year at the district), so you never knew how much that meant to me!
5. Cathy Bridge: What a pleasure to work with you! You are not only extremely competent but always available! Remember that time when we didn't send the GATE letters? You said you would always be supportive of me. Know that I am of you, as well!
6. Lesley Day: Those calls and chats have been extremely helpful. We make a great team as we balance each other! You make me a realistic optimist.
7. EUSD Cabinet and Principals: Tom (my very supportive boss), Kristi, Kelli, Ted, Melody, and Melissa. Principals and Vice Principals, I could not have asked for a better team! We have a lot of work to do, but joy comes from knowing that I have the blessing of working with all of you!
8. Darren (for taking care of Callie and me): Thank you for making sure I am fed and taking care of the house as I travel for work and decompression!
9. My family back home: My mom, my dad, my brothers, sister (in-law or by blood)—thank you for a great childhood and a great life!

These acknowledgments would not be complete without mentioning my eternal gratitude for the following inanimate objects: my 2015 Kia Soul (read chapter 5 and you'll know why!), my LG television and Prime Video subscription, my mirror, my notebook, my colored pens, my pillow, and boxes of recyclable paper towels.

Lastly, I would like to thank my unique self. I do deserve a hug.

Introduction

"When everything seems to be going against you, remember that the airplane takes off against the wind, not with it."

—Henry Ford

(Author: *Actually, it cannot fly unless wind flows against its wings during liftoff!*)

Have you wondered lately why you are still in this profession, still teaching and doing what you do in service of others? Have you been reflecting a lot on how certain attributes that you once found that made teaching enjoyable are *now making you unhappy*? Do you find yourself longing excessively for the weekend and those summers and breaks off? And here's the final determining question: Do you often feel exhausted...both emotionally and physically? If you answered yes to these questions—particularly the last one—you are heard, and there is a significant dose of empathy and compassion beaming at you right now.

I have occupied that mental space many times, particularly in the last three years, but also during my first year of teaching in the United States. This is the singular purpose for which this book was conceptualized and written. In a way, this book is meant to help the reader who is in a service-oriented field. I thank you for the blessing of listening to what my experiences have been like (yes, the references to third persons in this book were 90 percent my own experience!). I hope you take the time to self-reflect as you read each chapter and learn along the way.

I invite you to have plenty of Post-it Notes and perhaps a journaling notebook beside you as you read, as well! This will be reiterated again at the end of this introduction.

There is a serious problem with teacher/educator stress and anxiety, most acute during the last few years of this pandemic. A 2021 study by Ozamiz-Etxebarria et al. revealed that teachers are reporting worrisome levels of anxiety (17 percent), depression (19 percent), and stress (30 percent). Astonishingly, teachers from Asia report greater anxiety compared to other regions of the world. Perhaps accountability pressure is greater in that part of the world. Additionally, anxiety levels are higher for teachers in K–12 schools than those representing universities. This is not surprising. We can understand why, as our students present perhaps a greater level of challenges compared to the more self-sufficient students at colleges and universities. (I am teaching in a graduate program right now!)

Another study (de Oliveira Silva et al., 2021) indicates higher ranges of anxiety and levels of depression, up to 49 percent, and called for increased attention to the mental well-being of educators. I believe that in this profession, a toolbelt of effective coping strategies that are easy to deploy and does not exert a significant cost (in both funding and other resources) is needed. I also believe there should be a college course in every school of education in the country that teaches these sets of skills.

This book is about helping the teacher so he or she can help the student. However, it is not only for the teacher or educator, but also for those whose jobs are service-oriented and leave them drained at the end of the day. This exhaustion is different from just the physical feeling of tiredness; it is more often a feeling of incapacity and helplessness, of wanting to give up and just curl into a ball while eating Cheetos and chocolate donuts. It is emotional exhaustion, pure and simple—the type postulated to lead to burnout. If you have been feeling this way more than occasionally, this book will walk you through the whys and hows of addressing these feelings through the adoption of positive coping strategies that will hopefully become habits.

The last chapter of this book is about job satisfaction, which is serious business! You will not last more than three years if you are not finding joy in your job. Fortunately, there are factors that can help improve your job satisfaction, whether you are a teacher, a school staff member, or an administrator. The heart of this book aligns with my personal mission of helping individuals maintain a healthy dose of hope and optimism, as well as reclaim the joy of living the "work"—of recognizing one's "exhaustion triggers," developing an awareness for aspects of human nature that makes them feel this way and predisposes them to act a certain way, and employing simple strategies that get them thinking their way out of a gloomy "funk."

Each chapter revolves around a common theme—starting with defining *optimism* and delineating between its two forms. There is a chapter about humor—which you must have, even if you consider yourself humorless most of the time! This book will orient you toward certain biases in thinking we all possess—and will invite you to be aware of the times when your thinking veers that way, as your thoughts will influence your feelings and behaviors. There is also a chapter about explanatory styles (*How do you explain your own way of thinking about both pleasant and unpleasant events?*). I also hope you find easily actionable strategies within the chapter discussing decompression and detachment.

The book is oriented in such a way that you can hop around chapters and sections. You are also encouraged to do the following:

1. Have a notebook and colored pencils nearby so you can draw! (Sketchnoting is a way to better understand and remember). If you are unfamiliar with sketchnoting, there are many YouTube videos that show you how! When you are sketching, there is also a great probably you will get into this calm state of flow.
2. Have a stack of Post-it Notes handy and write an actionable item (one you can easily do) on each note.
3. Post these notes around your mirror, on your work computer, or near your workspace.
4. Invest in a karaoke microphone (you will learn why in chapter 5).
5. Be comfortable with screaming, and telling jokes, and looking deeply into your emotions. You are highly encouraged to talk to yourself most of the time as you are reading this book. It is recommended that you actually verbalize this conversation.
6. Always ensure your car has a full tank of gas—you might find yourself going three times around the neighborhood before coming home. Chapter 5 explains why!

Before you start reading the book, do the following:

1. Hug yourself. You have done an enormous amount of heavy lifting these past few years. You deserve a hug—just as tight as when you hug your students.
2. Face a mirror and notice how unique and beautiful you are! You truly are! How wonderful is it to contemplate that everything about you is unique!
3. Close your eyes. Take ten deep breaths (those that come from your tummy) and exhale slowly. Each breath is a reminder of how amazing it is to be alive and to have control over your thoughts, feelings, and actions.

Thank you for reading this book!

Chapter One

Defining Optimism and the Optimism Continuum

Why Is It More Than Just Positive Thinking?

A friend once said, likely quoting someone famous, that only during a very dark night can one see the stars. Hence, it can be quite challenging to imagine individuals interested in contemplating the construct of optimism during a raging pandemic. It is difficult to fathom any individual would also be interested in discussing hope, gratitude, and self-efficacy when they have apparently lost all control over conditions such as wearing a mask or ever traveling for pleasure again, and yet we must.

Doubtless, quarantine conditions, contact tracing, and countless news stories about overcrowded hospitals and new COVID variants constitutes an environment conducive to writing a book about optimism. It is, indeed, during the most challenging times that people will find it most difficult to imagine rosier, brighter outcomes, and yet one could argue that it is during these times that a significant dose of optimism is much needed.

Lewis Carroll famously stated, "Begin at the beginning and go on till you come to the end; then stop" (Brainy Quotes, 2020). Hence, a definition of optimism is needed. Fortunately, there is no dearth of definitions for the construct. But with such broad constructs lie difficulties associated with delineating it with similar psychological concepts, such as hope, gratefulness, and cheerfulness.

What is optimism? Here are a few descriptions curated from a simple internet engine search. *Merriam-Webster* (2020) provides a good, simple start:

1. *a doctrine that this world is the best possible world*
2. *an inclination to put the most favorable construction upon actions and events or to anticipate the best possible outcome*

Optimism is multidimensional in its scope; hence, it begs for greater elaboration. Consider the following additional descriptions:

1. "Optimism is a mental attitude characterized by hope and confidence in success and a positive future" (Scott, 2020 from VeryWellmind.com).
2. "Hopefulness: the attitude that good things will happen, and that people's wishes or aims will ultimately be fulfilled" (*American Psychological Association Dictionary*, 2020).
3. "Optimism is an individual difference variable that reflects the extent to which people hold generalized favorable expectancies for their future" (Carver, Scheier, and Segestrom, 2010).
4. Optimism is an "emotional and psychological perspective on life." An optimistic person exhibits a positive frame of mind and expects the best outcome from any given situation (AlleyDog.com, 2019).
5. Optimism is "an attitude that can positively affect a person's mental and physical health." Optimism may be helpful in alleviating a person's stress and increasing longevity. It is the belief that "outcomes of events or experiences will generally be positive" (*Psychology Today*, 2019).

From the descriptions above, it can be gleaned that optimism is an attitude, a belief, a confidence, a mindset, and a hope for positive future outcomes. A quote loosely attributed to Churchill—be forewarned that this attribution could turn out to be false as no record could be found that he truly uttered these words)—also reflects the idea that optimism and pessimism are worldviews: "A pessimist sees the difficulty in every opportunity; an optimist sees the opportunity in every difficulty." Positive psychologists argue for different types of optimism, reflecting a continuum:

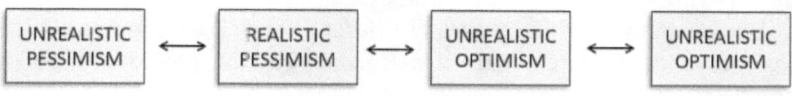

Figure 1.1. Pessimism—Optimism Continuum. Author created.

An unrealistic pessimist will consistently predict that future outcomes will be dire and that all actions taken in the present are for moot. This person will hence see no reason to engage in any effort or will most likely engage in risk-avoidance. Further, this person may also manifest significant loss-aversion. A realistic pessimist will still have a worldview that future outcomes are dire, but these individuals can take stock of the present, assess current realities, and still not find any positive data point to leverage for anticipating a rosier future. They tend to leverage negative events more than positive ones.

At the other end of the spectrum, an unrealistic optimistic is a person who adopts and applies positive thinking across any situation. Facing brutal facts is not an area of strength for this person. This individual may be unwilling to examine current realities, instead committing to a belief that phenomenally positive outcomes are to be expected. Hence, like the unrealistic pessimist, this individual may opt not to engage any effort.

Realistic optimism, the subject of this book, is sometimes called rational optimism, to emphasize the involvement of thinking. Realistic optimism, as explained by both Sneider (2001) and Degrandpre (2000), is the "tendency to maintain a positive outlook within the constraints of the available measurable phenomena situated in the physical and social world" (Beazley, 2009, http://positivepsychology.org.uk/the-many-sides-of-optimism/). The component of reality could easily be synthesized from this definition, as it factors into the construct a consideration of current knowledge and availability of resources, choices, and action options. Rational optimism is the goal, as there is no heavy weight attached to current and past negative events when positive future outcomes are considered. So, finally, here is the definition that will frame the context of the discussion in this book:

> *Realistic optimism is the attitude, belief, and confidence (A-B-C) that there is hope for favorable outcomes, upon consideration of present conditions and available options for actions.*

It can be difficult to distinguish among these different types of pessimism/optimism mindsets, so let's look at the different ways that individuals may feel about the COVID-19 pandemic. As you read about the different expressions of attitudes and beliefs, reflect on how you felt in early 2020.

Table 1.1. Thinking about the pandemic: From an unrealistic pessimist's view to an unrealistic optimist's unwarranted belief

Unrealistic Optimist	"There is no future for humankind. This virus will wipe us all out. I will most likely catch it, and if I don't die, I will most likely be debilitated from lingering illness."
Realistic Pessimist	"This virus is truly scary. It has killed a lot of people. Yes, there is a vaccine, but the vaccine is not foolproof, and it has a lot of significant and serious side effects—plus most people will probably not consider getting vaccinated anyway. The situation is hopeless—I might as well proceed as normal. I don't like wearing masks after all . . ."
Rational Optimist	"This pandemic is scary, and I know that hospitalization rates are up. I have studied how this virus spreads and what it does to the body. I know how to lower my risks by taking specific actions. I am positive that once vaccines are widely available, we can return to doing our favorite activities. In the meantime, I will continue wearing a mask, washing my hands, and educating myself."
Unrealistic Optimist	"This pandemic will soon be over! Cheer up! The future is bright—we just need to keep on engaging in positive thinking."

EXERCISE 1: Review the following two scenarios. Determine how a realistic/unrealistic pessimist/optimist might think about each situation and what courses of action each educator might engage depending on his/her mindset.

Scenario 1:	Scenario 2:
You were asked by your principal to provide a 20-minute presentation about a specific reading strategy. You delivered a lackluster presentation, with your peers appearing quite disengaged.	It is formal observation day for you but getting a speeding ticket on the day itself left you angry and discombobulated. You were hoping to "wow" your vice principal with a phenomenal lesson, but instead, you delivered the lesson in a confusing manner.

Figure 1.2. Exercise 1. Author created.

In both situations, the courses of action the educator takes is a consequence of the reflective thinking that is utilized. An unrealistic optimist will most possibly disregard any insights learned from the experience;

hence, they would miss the opportunity for growth. Adopting a philosophy of *"Declare victory and move forward!"* is not exactly beneficial for the educator. In some cases, the teacher might blame his or her peers when the presentation did not go as planned. Sometimes, the blame is placed on the students, who could be described as unmotivated, lacking self-regulation, or highly uncooperative (*"This is the most unprepared class of students I have ever taught!"*). The unrealistic optimist or pessimist might blame the teacher from the previous grade level (*"Well, obviously, the third-grade teacher failed at teaching them the prerequisite skills!"*), hence acknowledging no control over the situation.

Considering the second scenario, a realistic optimist might acknowledge that the root cause—getting a speeding ticket—led to the unfortunate, ineffective lesson delivery. While remaining confident that this one occurrence would not spell gloom and doom for all lesson delivery outcomes, the realistic optimist is able to consider actions that would solve the problem (i.e., *Do not overspeed!*). The realistic optimist does not shy away from analyzing what happened and what is happening, but he or she does not get stuck in forever ruminating on the bad event. The rational optimist can move forward and not be gripped with chronic feelings of defeat and hopelessness. Further, a rational optimist is also able to acknowledge that effort is necessary for future positive outcomes. Realistic optimism opens the mind to solutions and does not close the door to the contemplation of rosier futures.

Many individuals find it significantly challenging to associate present reality, which includes unpleasant events, and the persistent hope for good things. Realistic optimism takes hard work! It requires cognitive effort to "unclick" the mind so it can stop focusing on the negative event/s. A dose of courage and a positive self-concept (how an individual assesses her/himself) is required as the individual must confront brutal facts. Negative emotions such as shame and guilt might be involved (consider the two scenarios in the exercise). Unlike the irrational optimists, the rational optimists are less annoying and may experience less stress.

There are other reasons why irrational optimism is not the mindset to adopt. When optimism becomes unbounded, it can lead to unrealistic expectations, as well as risky actions, failure to practice safe behavior, and no attempts made to prepare for the future, which can even endanger one's life. Positivity can become toxic; a "good-thoughts-only" approach to life can lead to the rejection of negative emotions (this is an ineffective coping strategy) and a false façade. Individuals who reflect a "good-vibes-only" attitude may miss out on support when needed. Additionally, unrealistic optimism can result in significant pain and suffering when the rosy outcome is not realized.

All definitions of optimism invoke an individual's worldview about the future. However, as elaborated above, an evaluation of the present is critical in the strategies toolbox of the rational optimist. And this examination, putting the present in focus, can be accompanied by discomfort, as stated earlier:

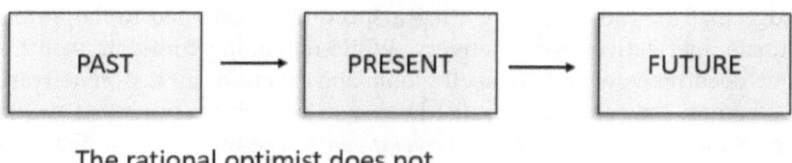

The rational optimist does not get stuck here.

Figure 1.3. The Rational Optimist's Path: A Rosy Future Starts with the Present (and Sometimes the Past). Author created.

The good news is realistic optimism can be learned. For most individuals, the most challenging stage in the process can be facing current negative experiences. As stated above, one's current reality may bring about suffering, loneliness, pain, and other negative emotions. The act of actively trying to find something positive about these experiences is also difficult. However, negative emotions are valuable. They signal the need for support, and they develop resilience. An individual may learn effective coping strategies from experiencing negative emotions. Plus, how can an individual feel the absolute joy of a positive outcome if one has never felt the unpleasant feelings of negative emotions?

Examining current realities may empower a person to be able to think with more clarity about what actions can be taken in the present to yield a more positive future. And yet, it is through the pandemic that spanned three years that educators realized the following "gifts":

1. **The gift of becoming more technology competent.** Many teachers were unceremoniously thrust into the world of remote teaching in

March 2020. All educators collectively proved they could rise to that challenge, and everyone's skills involving the use of instructional technology tools and devices have sharpened! Who could have predicted that all teachers would be able to engage students remotely? There were, it seemed, insurmountable challenges. But there were so many insights, as well, as to what makes lessons engaging.

2. **Increased focus on mental wellness.** Everyone suddenly realized how important it is, as educators, to put a premium on one's mental well-being—as well as the well-being of the students! Suddenly, instructional minutes were devoted to emotional check-ins and breathing exercises, without educators (hopefully) feeling guilty about robbing minutes away from English language arts and math. Inaccurately labeled "soft skills" (such as self-control, resilience, and motivation) became very important skills and took center stage!

3. **The realization that connectedness can still be preserved and built.** Though it is truly lamentable that educators and students could not hug each other or even meet face-to-face in groups larger than two (yes, that is an attempt at humor), we discovered that we could "meet" virtually. And yes, it was proven that smiles *can* be transmitted through one's eyes—and this kind of smile is better anyway! Individuals also became creative at replacing common greetings like handshakes with foot bumps and finger gestures (from six feet away)!

From examining collective suffering through the last three years, these experiences can be leveraged to empower ourselves to problem-solve, to make our current reality better (finding joy in the simplest things), and to believe in a brighter future. It may seem like during the pandemic, individuals lost so much control. However, it can be argued that collectively, we learned that many things were within our control. As a society, we also learned the importance of caring for each other. As educators, and as a community, an increased awareness for misinformation was developed. Collectively, filtering misinformation by using reliable and valid sources was one of the key skills learned.

The most humorous insight, perhaps, is that during the pandemic, our society also was taught valuable lessons in biology, virology, and epidemiology without having to go back to high school and pay for college! If one is a realistic optimist, even during the quarantine and when case rates were off the charts, people were able to keep an open mind, understanding the following distinct possibilities: (1) We will evolve more effective therapies for other viruses; (2) Science will continue to investigate and design better vaccines; (3) The next time a pandemic happens (and surely there will be a second or third or *nth* one), we will be a world that is better prepared.

Here are more pandemic blessings that should be cause for reflection for the rational optimist. Savor the joy of ticking each statement as it applies to you:

1. Most individuals, once addicted to ordering food, *relearned* how to cook. Many recognized the value of cooking their own food, as eating healthy became easier.
2. During quarantine, individuals reclaimed hobbies that brought them joy. Some began cross-stitching again (even during Zoom meetings!). A few educators I know watched obscene numbers of YouTube video tutorials on effective remote teaching, and more teachers controlled their own professional growth by signing up for virtual webinars.
3. Most individuals discovered a closer association with nature. Suddenly, "forest bathing" (the practice of getting wonderfully lost among the trees) became popular. When gyms closed, many found the outdoors to be the safest places to exercise, and hence they rekindled their lost relationships with nature.
4. Teachers and healthcare staff became superheroes! Those who worked in the service industry became *non-invisible*! People suddenly realized the hard work and dedicated service that educators (and healthcare workers and service staff) offered to society.
5. Working from home became an alternative, and virtual meetings allowed people to connect. The pandemic proved that some workers *can* actually work remotely without any significant loss in productivity or effectiveness of service. Individuals were provided opportunities to be closer to family and pets and reduce carbon emissions and time wasted by no longer commuting through traffic. In the education world, parents who were working were provided opportunities to meet with teachers at times formerly inconvenient for them, via virtual meetings.

THE BENEFITS OF BECOMING RATIONAL OPTIMISTS

It is not surprising that optimism, of the rational kind, is associated with several positive health outcomes. According to a 2008 article from Harvard Medical School (online publication), optimism improves overall health and may lead to a longer life. Referencing a 1960s study, pessimism scores were linked to higher mortality rates—i.e., the higher the score on the pessimism scale, the higher the rate of mortality. In another more recent study referenced in the article, the most pessimistic individuals were found to manifest a 42 percent higher mortality rate than the most optimistic individuals. Note that this is a correlation study, and not proof that optimism directly causes longer lives. However, in a 2019 meta-analysis study, Rosanzi et al. confirmed the association between optimism and cardiovascular health; the conclusion was that more optimistic individuals suffered fewer incidences of cardiovascular disorders. So simply allowing oneself to think about probable positive outcomes can result in health benefits!

Because optimism can be learned (and pessimism unlearned), these studies provide insights on how interventions can be designed to boost optimism levels and reap cardiovascular benefits. Many studies (for an excellent review, consider reading Scheier and Carver's 2018 review) verify the numerous positive associations between health variables and optimism. Among the health variables influenced by optimism are blood pressure, anxiety, surgery recovery, depression, sleep quality/problems, and rehospitalization. Perhaps the most relevant research for educators on optimism is its impact on stress. Studies indicate that realistic optimism can buffer against chronic stress and is also associated with the implementation of more effective coping strategies. Feeling stressed right now? Just think about how tomorrow can most possibly be better than today!

There is an argument to be made for teaching realistic optimism to students. It has been shown that those with higher levels of optimism manifest increased motivation, self-efficacy, goal-orientation, and cooperation. There are less risks for anxiety and depression, as well!

ACTIVITY: *I NOTICE . . . I WONDER!*

Instructions: Think about a friend or relative who was a realistic optimist during the pandemic. *What did you notice about this individual? What did you wonder?* Now, think about a friend or relative who was an unrealistic optimist during the pandemic. *What did you notice about this individual? What did you wonder?*

MEASURING OPTIMISM

It can be presumed that optimism, because of its multidimensional nature, may be challenging to measure. Psychologists have developed and validated several scales for measuring the construct. The scales utilized for measuring optimism levels were developed through the adoption of two perspectives. The first perspective requires an approach that measures an individual's expectations of his or her future. Hence, this perspective aims to determine the tendency of an individual to have bright or gloomy expectations about the future. The second approach utilizes attributional or explanatory styles (more about this construct will be discussed in later chapters). A person's attributional style refers to how he or she explains the causes of a bad or good event.

One of the scales used to measure optimism is the Life-Orientation Test (LOT), also commonly referred to as the optimism scale (M.F. Scheier, C.S. Carver, and M.W. Bridges, 1994). This tool provides individuals with an indication of their optimism level. The test is fortunately quite short, consisting of ten items that aim to distinguish the person's placement in the pessimism-optimism continuum. Respondents rate their degree of agreement on a Likert-scale: 0 = strongly disagree, 1 = disagree, 2 = neutral, 3 = agree, and 4 = strongly agree. A recent version of this scale includes twelve items where four are worded positively, four are worded negatively, and hence, reverse-scored, and four fillers. Check out the items in the revised scale below. Note that items 2, 5, and 6 are fillers, and those marked R are reverse-scored. This test is available to the public on the Positive Psychology website (https://positivepsychology.com/life-orientation-test-revised/).

Try determining your own optimism level by answering the following questions using the scale described above:

Table 1.2.

Item No.	Statement	Score
1.	In uncertain times, I usually expect the best.	
2.	It is easy for me to relax. (N)	
3.	If something can go wrong for me, it will. (R)	
4.	I always look on the bright side of things.	
5.	I am always optimistic about my future.	
6.	I enjoy my friends a lot. (N)	
7.	It is important for me to keep busy. (N)	
8.	I hardly ever expect things to go my way. (R)	
9.	Things never work out the way I want them to. (R)	
10.	I don't get upset too easily. (N)	
11.	I am a believer in the idea that "every cloud has a silver lining."	
12.	I rarely count on good things to happen to me. (R)	
	For all items not marked with an N or R, responding '0' would denote a rating of '0' and responding '4' would align with a score of '4.' For items marked R, which measure pessimism, a score of '0' would add a rating of '4,' a response of '1' would add a score of '3,' and it continues accordingly. Do not score items marked N.	
Sum up your score here		

The scores (last row) provide an estimate of how optimistic or pessimistic you are (remember that pessimism and optimism lie in a continuum). Find your score in the table below:

Table 1.3.

Score Range	Interpretation
0–13	Low Optimism (High Pessimism)
14–18	Moderate Optimism
19–24	High Optimism (Low Pessimism)

How did you score? Were you surprised at the results? Do you have a future-orientation that is geared toward more positive outcomes? If you are an educator, how do you think the most challenging and struggling students in your class would score? More importantly, as an educator, are you a realistic optimist? Does it matter to you?

Go back and analyze how you responded to each item. In particular, how did you answer item 1? Most of the items on this scale reflect the future-orientation perspective—how an individual forecasts the future. If you scored in the low optimism range, ask yourself why you have an expectation of a gloomy future. What evidence (from current reality) do you have that the future will not turn out to be favorable? Question the validity of what you listed as evidence. How about having your students complete the scale (anonymously, if needed)? How do you think they would score?

CHAPTER 1 HOMEWORK

Have you ever watched the *SNL* (*Saturday Night Live*) skits titled "Debbie Downer"? Are you a Debbie Downer yourself? Try watching several episodes on YouTube. Watch it with your friends and family. You might be surprised to find yourself thinking about a family member, a colleague, a friend, or even yourself in a particular situation, when that person reflects Debbie Downer's language and action.

> Are you a Debbie Downer? Do you occasionally (albeit unwittingly) drain others' energy by focusing on potential negative outcomes?
> Do you know of a Debbie Downer? How do you respond?

Figure 1.4. Author created.

CHAPTER 1 KEY MESSAGES

- Optimism is not just positive thinking. It's a way of viewing the world and believing that positive outcomes are possible.
- Optimism occurs in a spectrum, from unrealistic pessimism to unrealistic optimism. A person's level of optimism may vary, but it is often quite stable.

- A realistic optimist is an individual who is optimistic about future outcomes but who grounds this belief in reality (keeping their eyes wide open!).
- Facing the brutal facts or the harsh realities of the present (if these exist) is a prerequisite for cultivating realistic optimism.
- Negative emotions are not "bad" emotions. Although these constitute negative feelings, they serve to intensify positive emotions.
- Unrealistic optimism is an unhealthy condition. It may lead to improbable expectations and promote risky behaviors.
- Optimism can be measured using a scale. Try answering some of the items on page XX. Do you possess low, average, or high levels of optimism?
- Do you want to view examples of unhealthy, unrealistic pessimism? Watch old Debbie Downer episodes on *SNL*'s YouTube channel and have a laugh!

Chapter Two

The Negativity Bias
Classroom Manifestations and Ways of Addressing

In chapter 1, the psychological construct of optimism was explored, defined, and elaborated on. A case was argued for promoting and inspiring (through learning and teaching via modeling and explicit instruction) the brand of optimism referred to as realistic, as opposed to unrealistic optimism. In this chapter, several cognitive biases or wired ways of thinking will be discussed and explored to enable the reader to understand why the adoption of an optimistic mindset could be challenging. These mental shortcuts can often sabotage a person's rational reflection of an event and consequently may lead to irrational feelings and actions.

This chapter will include discussions of multiple constructs and fascinating ideas in psychology, particularly human cognition and behavior. Some of these concepts are quite surprising: They provide insights into human nature. Teachers, administrators, and other educators will no doubt find this chapter meaningful, as it lays bare the case as to why learning to be optimistic requires consistent effort and commitment, and the reason falls (failures) are common and to be expected. This chapter will also provide ideas for cultivating optimism through planned efforts or opportunities to reset thinking and behavior.

COGNITIVE BIASES

According to the website VeryWellMind.com, a *cognitive bias* is a thinking error that occurs during the processing and interpretation of information. This faulty way of thinking, hypothesized to be hardwired, has consequences that may be undesirable, as it influences decisions and behaviors. Why do these biases exist? Psychologists postulate these faulty ways of thinking are the result of the brain's attempt to simplify information perception and interpretation, as we are bombarded with information overload every second of our existence. These automatic pathways of thinking make the process more efficient—reducing cognitive load, or the effort we expend when we think about information received, considering the amount of information we receive! Additionally, decision-making is achieved in a faster way. One can think of cognitive biases as thinking shortcuts!

Psychologists categorize these biases into two kinds—some are associated with memory, or how a person may remember or perceive an event. The other category of biases is related to addressing attention challenges. This latter category makes sense, as a person is limited in his or her attention resources (and as teachers, we are often subject to an onslaught of information ourselves while performing our jobs). There are many known biases, but we will focus on two that are the most pertinent to the topic of this book—the Optimism Bias and the Negativity Bias.

Optimism Bias: How Can This Even Exist?

Interestingly, psychologists have found that people are actually predisposed to be too optimistic for their own good (this is called the optimism bias). This concerns people's view of outcomes and estimation of the likelihood of negative events happening. It turns out that individuals do anticipate more likely better outcomes and underestimate potential failures. This may suggest that teachers could be biased in estimating how well their students will perform on a test, or how good their teaching evaluations will turn out. It can be assumed there will be attendant behaviors that may result from this skewed outlook. However, this cognitive bias does not suggest that people in general have an overall sunny outlook on their lives.

The optimism bias seems counterintuitive to what we know about human nature, *but it exists*. Essentially, people with an optimism bias will underestimate the likelihood of negative events happening (*"I will not fail the Algebra test!"* or *"My class will not have a problem behaving appropriately during the field trip!"*), and they will overestimate the occurrence of a positive event (*"I will rock that faculty presentation!"* or *"I will have everything ready for the field trip next week!"*). This mental shortcut is made regardless of the current realities. Not surprisingly, this bias can lead to poor decision-making, which can then yield unproductive (sometimes disastrous) behaviors. We see the optimism bias manifested in education—from the classroom to the district office—and no one is immune! Review the following examples and reflect on other ways in which this bias may show up.

Table 2.1.

Optimistic (Biased) Thinking	Actions
1. Student: *I will get an A on my ten-page essay assignment.*	Student does not engage in effort, spending his/her weekend playing video games.
2. Teacher: *I will just "wing" that lesson through, I am good at thinking on the spot.*	Delivery of lesson is ineffective as no preparation and/or planning was done.
3. School Leader: *My school's math scores will rise! We will most likely see a narrowing of the achievement gap because of the new math program we purchased.*	No comprehensive study of the math program was made before its purchase. Teacher feedback was not sought, no pilot or trial was done, and no professional development was provided.

The optimism bias is also referred to as the illusion of the absence of vulnerability leading to potentially risky behaviors. This bias is widespread and appears to be *culture agnostic*, although there may be gender differences (females are reported as being more cautiously optimistic in research regarding economic status). Individuals who refuse to wear seat belts, who overly spend on gambling tickets, who believe their children are specifically gifted, or who underestimate the risks of a procedure may be manifesting an optimism bias. In the education workplace, an individual who frequently volunteers may possess such bias, as the likelihood of success when one is stretched too thin is decreased—but the person overestimates his or her chances of delivering a quality service or product.

> **REFLECTION QUESTION**
> How do you manifest the optimism bias? Think of a specific situation when you tended thought that a rosy outcome was far more likely to happen and was proven wrong! How did it make you behave?

Figure 2.1. Author created.

The Negativity Bias and Loss Aversion

If there is a bias for thinking optimistically, there is also a well-researched and documented bias for anticipating or overly thinking about negative experiences. Think of the following: Do you often find yourself ruminating on past mistakes? Do you continuously relieve the negative emotions you felt due to unpleasant experiences in the past? Do you have a problem avoiding fixating on negative news? If you answered yes, you, like many individuals on earth, may have a negativity bias.

Psychologists define the negativity bias as the tendency of individuals to perceive negative stimuli more readily—a greater sensitivity for negative events than positive ones. This faulty way of thinking can exert a powerful effect on thoughts, judgments, decisions, and behaviors. There are two operations involved in the negativity bias: (1) a tendency to register negative stimuli more readily (increased receptiveness), and (2) a propensity to recall and dwell on these negative events (rumination).

The negativity bias is a double-edged sword, and it can lead to unhappiness, stress, and emotional exhaustion. Because of the negativity bias, criticisms (or perceptions of such) deliver a more painful sting to the psyche than the pleasure felt from a praise, even though the praise most likely outnumber the stings. This cognitive bias can help explain how negative first impressions are so challenging to erase, and why past negative experiences can have such long-lasting effects. Negative experiences are more easily recalled, dwelled on, and remembered vividly. Review the table below and evaluate whether you have engaged in the examples provided:

Your Inner Critic can...
- Be loud!
- Be excessively negative
- Trigger unwarranted stress
- Be downright cruel and mean!
- Rob you of joy ☹

Figure 2.2. Author created.

Table 2.2.

The negativity bias causes us to . . .	So as educators, we . . .
• Remember sad or painful experiences better than pleasant ones.	Recall all the times we had classroom management issues (e.g., a student talking back) and forget about all the times we have perfectly smooth-running classrooms.
• Recall criticisms more readily than praise.	Remember when our principal five years ago criticized an observed lesson and not recall the many times we received praise from this same principal, fellow teachers, and students.
• Respond more strongly to negative events.	Cry our eyes out for not having been selected as site teacher of the year, discounting the many times when our actions were celebrated at meetings.
• Think about negative experiences more frequently than about positive ones.	Ruminate on those sad instances when our students were quite disrespectful when 99 percent of the class remained engaged and joyful about learning.
• React more intensely to negative events than to equally positive ones.	Display negative emotions more frequently than relishing positive emotions.

The negativity bias can help decrease a person's motivation to engage in effort to complete a task. Imagine the impact of this bias on students with disadvantaged life experiences—and how this can lead to further disengagement from effort that will actually address the problem. The same reasoning applies for the teacher who may possess a significant negativity bias—a manifestation could be decreased motivation to achieve a goal. Negativity bias adversely influences resilience, and since teaching is a highly stressful endeavor, a way of thinking that is more highly attuned to negative stimuli can hamper the engagement of more effective and active stress-management coping skills.

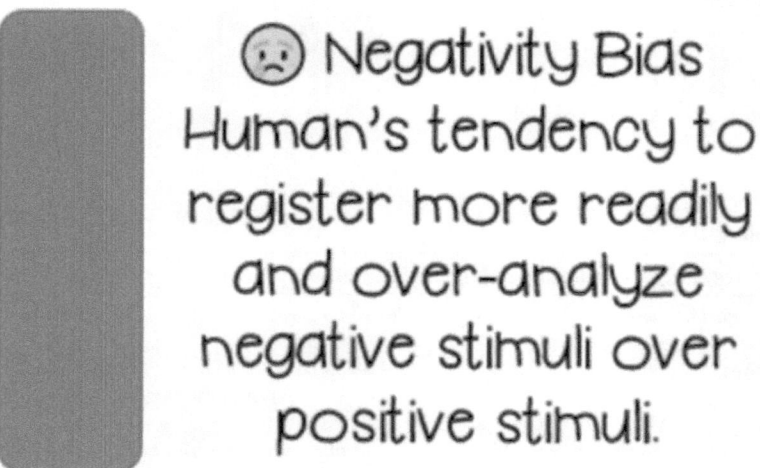

Figure 2.3. Author created.

Loss Aversion and FOLO: Fear of Losing Out

It turns out that not only do humans tend to perceive, react, and remember more intensely negative events, but we also have a deep fear of losing out. This is a construct known in psychology as loss aversion, the strong response (usually in the form of fear) to losing anything—tangible or not. Loss aversion might explain why we are hyper-focused on our setbacks compared to our successes. As Charles Darwin so eloquently expressed, "Everyone feels blame more acutely than praise" (cited from *Psychology Today*, Heshmat, 2018). *Do you agree?*

Notable psychological studies have shown that we get more annoyed losing $10 than we become joyful upon finding $10. Another study showed that participants were more inclined to consider surgery as a treatment when told that the operation was 70 percent successful, than when they were informed that in 30 percent of the cases, the surgery was unsuccessful. Psychologists hypothesize that losing is twice as painful as gains that make a person feel good. Hence, the 5:1 equation is offered when giving praises versus criticisms: *Five kind comments are needed to balance out one critical remark!* We do this for our students and friends. Hence, let's be intentional about doing it for ourselves, as well. This is also helpful to commit to when engaging in self-talk.

In a study by Levin et al. (2002), participants were asked to choose between two activities: (1) create a basic pizza by adding ingredients like sausage and pepperoni, or (2) work from a fully loaded pizza and remove any other ingredients. Not surprisingly, participants who were asked to remove ingredients had difficulty doing just that and ended up with a significantly more loaded pizza than the other group. Loss aversion predicted that the loss from removing ingredients is more intensely felt than adding ingredients! Think about the following: When looking at your schedule, why is it so difficult to remove events than create them? Why do you always have to be part of every school committee and then have a hard time giving up some commitments? Why do you feel the urge to volunteer for some committee when you already have three? When developing lesson plans, why is it so easy to overpack activities and so painful to give up some tasks? Could this be the solution to overdecorated classrooms? Start with blank walls each year and build off from there, because plucking off materials from the board may be more painful and more intensely felt! Now think about how this applies to grading!

FOMO: Fear of Missing (Losing) Out

Fear of missing out refers to the perception that everyone else possesses more and has better life experiences and opportunities than you. This leads to negative emotions, such as sadness and frustration, as well as uneasiness and stress. FOMO can also cause individuals to behave in potentially risky ways to try to achieve and obtain what others seem to have. The negative feelings resulting from FOMO can be *all-consuming*. It can be argued that this is an extension of the negativity bias and loss aversion. FOMO leads to lower scores on the mental well-being and life satisfaction scale.

It can be hypothesized that educators (teachers and administrators) may constantly experience FOMO due to the tighter social connectedness of staff in schools. Schools operate like a close-knit family. Do administrators, teachers, and other staff members at school have the competency to stop and question their beliefs and perceptions? As a teacher, do you often feel anxious about perceptions that students in Mrs. X's class seem to have more fun than your students, and that students in Mr. Y appear to learn more (compared to yours)? Or perhaps, you suffer from comparisons you make with yourself and other educators about your own instructional or leadership competencies.

If you are a district administrator, do you compare yourself relentlessly with others? If you learn that Dr. X or Mr. Y came to work on two consecutive Saturdays, do you feel the need to *hustle* as much? If you are a site administrator, if you noticed that Mr. X in a nearby school consistently serves his staff with coffee and donuts every Wednesday, do you feel the need to keep up, perhaps even add more? Does this constant state of comparisons to a perceived higher standard supposedly exhibited by others leave you feeling helpless and unhappy?

Has FOMO/FOLO propelled you to accept every invitation to professional social events, which you actually detest (you know, those events where fake awards are handed out and you have to smile and fake-clap—those events where you must "meet and greet" with strangers while sipping free wine in the name of networking)? Do you fear you would be losing out on opportunities when past experiences indicate that these events are truly a waste of time? It might be time to just say no and prioritize your well-being. But if you do, are you subsequently assailed by feelings of FOMO, wondering what everyone else is doing while you choose to sit it out?

Hopefully, you will finally recognize FOMO for what it is—a way to also avoid feeling negative emotions such as shame and guilt. In these situations, take the moment to question whether you are truly going to miss a great opportunity for learning and growth. Be specific about what you feel you will exactly miss. Will you derive joy from engaging in the task or attending the event? Engage in a cost-benefit analysis: Is the opportunity equal to just reading a book on the subject? Is the opportunity worth sacrificing your personal-wellness or family time?

Commit to only succumbing to FOLO if the event or opportunity will truly contribute significantly to your professional and personal growth and your happiness, and if there is no actual viable or better alternative.

FREE YOURSELF FROM THE NEGATIVITY BIAS AND FOMO

Because educators do not need to feel additional stress or be burdened with more negative emotions (shame, guilt, sadness, recriminations) in their lives, there is a need for them to equip themselves with proactive measures to mitigate the negativity bias and FOMO. Fortunately, psychologists have suggestions on how to manage this. For each suggestion (adapted from VeryWellMind.com, 2022—this is a *phenomenal website*!), an example will be provided to illustrate how this might manifest in the world of the school and classroom.

Arrest Negative Self-Talk

You must constantly evaluate what you say to yourself. Examine the kinds of thoughts that frequently course through your mind. At the end of your day, do you find yourself castigating your own actions? Unfortunately, many people do this all the time. It is not unusual to find oneself focusing on that one single event (e.g., the first ten minutes during Period 2) when the lesson did not go as planned. Do you berate yourself by thinking, *Why did I do that? What a stupid, stupid thing to do!* while driving home? When these thoughts pop up, stop and ask yourself: *Is it truly as bad as I think it is? Is my whole teaching career going to crash, will I lose my credentials, will I go homeless, or is the world going to collapse?* Then end with: *What can I do next time to problem-solve?* Or just ask: *What if things actually turn out well?* Then *move on!*

Try Reframing the Situation

Because of the negativity bias, we tend to view experiences and events through a dark, gloomy lens. When reflecting on your day, pay attention to how you describe the narrative: Are you focusing on an interpretation that is unnecessarily negative? Is this the *only* way you can view the event? Are you only recalling and processing the negative attributes of the experience and *leaving out* the positive? The capacity to reframe is very useful when you are processing challenging events. Here is a personal example recounted by a colleague...

She remembered a particular day when she participated in a very contentious parent meeting about a nonperforming, disengaged student. Driving home, she replayed the event repeatedly in her mind, agonizing over what she said and the negative responses she received from the parent .(Yes, the parent accused the teacher of not doing her job!) In her nth recounting of the meeting (she only had a forty-minute drive home), she suddenly stopped and committed to thinking about those things that were positive that she was leaving out and not considering: The meeting actually ended well because everyone had come up with a feasible plan of action. She made three (*not one, but three!*) well-received suggestions to the plan. While the parent was putting the blame on her, her principal bravely and successfully stopped the offensive tirade. The principal even managed to defend the teacher by pointing out evidence contrary to what the parent was expostulating. Hey, those were celebrations, and she needed to focus on those!

In reframing, an individual replaces the lens from which he or she is viewing the situation in a negative light. The exercise is akin to "rehashing the story," but it is accomplished differently—by adopting a positive lens. One might call this technique "remixing" the story. Thoughtful intent and awareness must be exercised before unpleasant ruminations start. As in the example above, it takes effort to break the scene, like a movie clip, minute by minute to find evidence of positive happenings. This might be challenging as the rumination cycle proceeds unchecked—and rehashing is often done multiple times!

Reframing Exercises

1. **Change from a passive mindset to an active mindset.** Instead of thinking, "*I really failed on that presentation*," shift to "*What is one small action I can take to deliver a better presentation next time?*" This does not mean avoiding the recognition that something unpleasant or negative happened, but it means shifting to a more action-oriented mindset.
2. **Move away from negative emotions to positive emotions.** From thinking, "*I hate to collaborate on this project, and not with those*

teachers!" move to "*What joyful activity can I contribute? Perhaps I can create the poster because I love art so much!*" Notice how such a shift immediately seems to feel a lot better.
3. **Abandon the deficit perspective.** Instead of counting all the little steps or areas you consider you are not good at, reframe those "deficits" as potential strengths. How might weathering these upsets in life be a blessing?
4. **Abandon the past and embrace the future.** Acknowledge the past ("*I am not good at teaching writing; hence my lessons are ineffective!*"), but imagine a better future ("*If I become better at being a teacher of writing, what would that look like? What would I be doing and feeling? How would my students react?*"). Then proactively list the steps you can take to make that vision a reality and the resources (time, materials, people) you can utilize.
5. **Shift your perspective from "others" to "self."** This will be very difficult for the educator. Instead of thinking this way: "*My students do not like me. And that parent hates me,*" shift to asking: "*What attributes do I like about myself? What do I like about my teaching?*" or "*In my interaction with the parent, what words did I say that I particularly like or that yielded a positive response?*" or "*What actions did I engage in that were helpful?*"

In the case of reframing, practice makes perfect. It may help to use your hands to force yourself to reframe. With your fingers, form a square with which you can pretend to view the situation differently. Do it several times! See how your thinking changes. Sketchnoting also helps. Sketch the "reframed" situation. Put in comment or thought bubbles! Pencil in feelings. Reframing "awakens" the joys that you did not feel when participating in the situation.

Engage a Pattern of Activities That Replaces the Negative Mindset

It can be challenging to "unclick" your mind when you are engaged in a cycle of negative ruminations and self-chastisements. However, consider developing a habit of stopping yourself and look for another activity that will calm your frazzled mind. Consciously direct your mental energy to doing something that pulls you out of your negative mindset. Find an activity that is pleasant and brings you joy. Here are some examples: baking, going for a walk, watching reruns of Hallmark holiday romances, or cross-stitching! One favorite guilty pleasure of a friend of mine is watching YouTube videos of celebrities without makeup (which she claims makes her feel better—perhaps because of FOMO) or the most embarrassing moments of the Kardashians. Another friend admits to feeling a tad guilty replacing his negative ruminations with a healthy dose of *schadenfreude*—finding joy in one's misfortune by watching videos of people caught doing questionable actions (like jumping off two flights of stairs). Somehow, for most people, the thought that even rich and powerful celebrities have bad moments helps to ground them.

Savor Positive Moments

Set aside time (for most, at the end of the day works well) and make it a habit to always recall positive moments to be savored. Reflecting on even the tiniest positive experience of the day allows you to recognize that these moments do exist, and you might be surprised to learn that there are a lot of them. Make an effort to develop this habit. A fellow middle-school science teacher reserved 4:30–5:00 p.m. as her PPR (*Pausing for Positive Reflections*) time. This also coincided with her drive time. Mrs. XM maintained that it was difficult, as every time she thought of a positive event, the dreaded word "but" would rear its ugly head at the end of the sentence. See examples she shared below:

- Johnny *actually perked up* today and participated in discussion . . . **BUT** he still did not submit his assignment.
- Principal R *actually smiled* at me today and stopped to greet me and say "good morning" . . . **BUT** she still has not acknowledged my work on the school spelling contest.
- Mr. S (another science teacher) returned my clean beakers and test tubes this morning . . . **BUT** he still has left my trays unwashed.

The word *but* signals that the individual is negating the positive moments that he or she is trying to savor and arrests any smile that should have come from feeling joyful. So, whenever you are feeling this word *but* coming on, you should remember to stop and arrest those thoughts.

This word should have no place in a PPR time. Later in this book, another strategy, called the 10-minute worry time (WT), will be explained. This is where you can actually use this word, ***but***, string as many of them as long and frequently in sentences and phrases as you would like!

Stop Catastrophizing

Research indicates that women might be more prone to catastrophize—which means magnifying negative incidents into possibly hurricane-level-10 events. A small error at work is easily magnified into a future most-probably-catastrophic event. Let me illustrate with a personal example shared by a friend: 1. Principal walked into the classroom when students were noisy (and some were quite rowdy and disengaged). 2. Teacher immediately engaged in some catastrophic thoughts, going from *I will be written up!* to *I will lose my teaching license!* and finally, *Then I'll be forced to go home as my H1B visa will be revoked . . .* , and consequently, *My kids will starve!* It is comedic when you can recount and have the time to look back and analyze, but those thoughts, to the person involved at that instant, were frightening.

Surprisingly, many people are very adept at catastrophizing. For parents, somehow every negative moment can easily be traced to an assured outcome: *My kids will starve!* or *We will be homeless!* As stated above, the sentence strings sound ridiculous, but when you are caught up in the cycle of imagining the world collapsing, it is quite difficult to arrest your thoughts and think logically. Can you imagine how children

> CATASTROPHIZATION
> This refers to thoughts that lead an individual to conclude that the worst possible outcome will happen, regardless of present conditions.

Figure 2.4. Author created.

or students must feel when as adults, who should know better, we still engage in this act?

What is the solution? Try to stop yourself at the very first thought in the sequence of catastrophic beliefs. This might include trying to think rationally about the imagined consequences. This might even lead to the individual laughing! Example: How can a rowdy classroom during one period (actually, five minutes) in one particular day result in the loss of a science instructor's teaching license? Is this the most rational, likely thing that will happen?

When you recognize that a catastrophizing cycle is about to commence, try to invoke the image of a wonderful superhero called Catastrophe Callie. This woman is dressed in a cape and some powerful boots as she can leap from a normal situation to a calamity in a single bound! Invoking this image inside one's head can be a reminder to laugh at yourself because you are being overly dramatic. There is an old video on YouTube called *What Could Be Worse?* and it is an exercise at using catastrophization to find joy and elicit a few good laughs. Try to find it and watch it!

Chapter Three

Realistic Optimism and Explanatory Styles

In the first chapter, it was reiterated that perceptions and beliefs about the present are as critical to developing an optimistic mindset as are thoughts about the future. It was discussed that the way an individual perceives, reflects on, and processes current realities (including how one explains how all of these interfaces with past events) may determine one's level of optimism. As an exercise, let's begin this chapter by having you reflect on how you would evaluate (rationalize) the following events and what strategies you would use to cope or move forward.

1. You were late for an important faculty meeting, and the district superintendent and other important district office staff members were there as guests.
2. You forgot instructional materials at home and hence, you got flustered while delivering a lesson that was being recorded and observed for training.
3. During a presentation you were giving, you saw several, glaring typographical errors, but it was too late to fix them!
4. In the middle of a math lesson, you found that you solved a few problems erroneously, getting the wrong answer (and *one of your students* pointed it out loudly in front of the whole class!).

Life will always consist of positive (pleasant ups) and negative (unpleasant downs) events. This roller coaster of events is normal. How an individual makes sense of the up and down events, and consequently act on them (cope with them), is referred to as his or her *explanatory style*. As an example, a brilliant math colleague recounted an unpleasant experience—event #4 (above)—all while being formally observed by the principal. You can probably guess that this equated to constant castigations toward himself for making such a "stupid" mistake. Feelings of shame and guilt lingered with the colleague for days.

Embarrassment caused reluctance to report to his class and teach the following day. He even utilized a "personal necessity" day, which, as reported, was spent in more depressive thoughts, as he engaged in replaying the event over and over in his mind, with copious amounts of blame for himself for carelessness, lack of attention and focus, and just plain stupidity (as he referred to it). Being the king of catastrophizing (take the time to read the chapter before this if you are unfamiliar with the term), he allowed event #4 to even disrupt his sleep, and the self-beleaguered colleague soon was caught up in excessive worry, unrealistic thoughts of losing his teaching license, and worse, fear of being transferred out of the district! This a manifestation of a "gloom and doom," pessimistic explanatory style can be quite consuming and negatively affect a person's life.

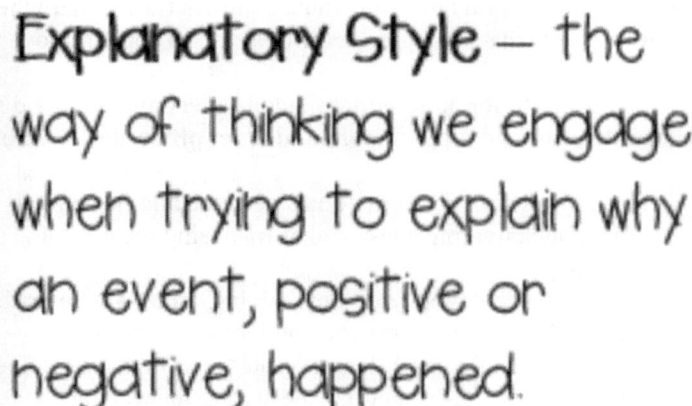

Figure 3.1. Author created.

EXPLANATORY STYLE AND ITS DIMENSIONS

The default explanation, explanatory style, that each of us engages to explain why a positive or negative event has occurred is apparently quite stable in our personalities—i.e., we engage the same style of thinking consistently. When trying to make sense of the ups and downs of life, individuals tend to rely on the same pattern of thinking. People employ the same general reasons across different events. It is not surprising that one's explanatory style can influence how stressful an event is viewed.

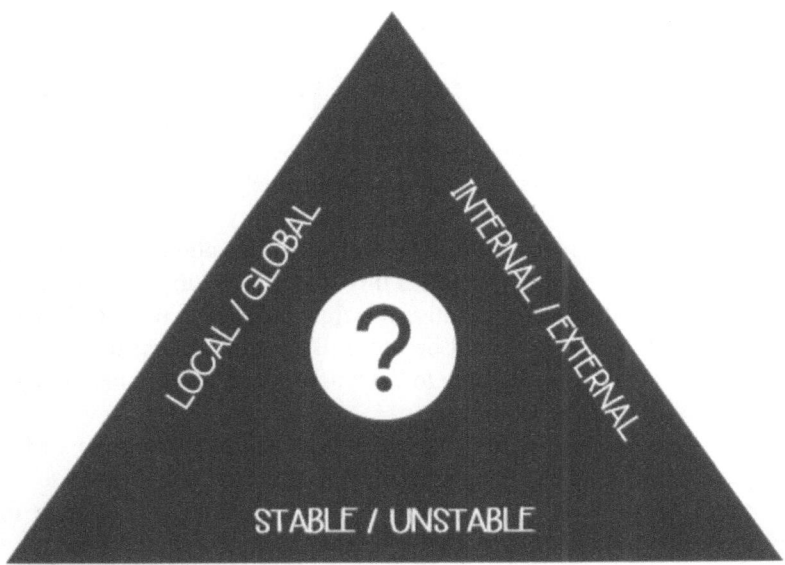

How do you explain negative events?

Figure 3.2. Author created.

The motivation to engage in problem-solving actions is also influenced by one's explanatory style. The father of positive psychology, Dr. Martin Seligman (2008, from www.PostivePsychology.com), identifies two explanatory styles: optimistic and pessimistic. To determine what kind of explanatory style you have, three dimensions or parameters are used to explain the cause (*and*, by extension, predict the consequences and choose the actions to be employed):

- Is the cause local or global?
- Is the cause stable or unstable?
- Is the cause internal or external?

These parameters can more easily be understood by remembering that these three dimensions are words that start with the letter *P*: *Pervasiveness*, *Permanence*, and *Personalization*.

1. P_1—**Pervasiveness:** Is the cause of the event seen as being *ever-present* in your life? Is this cause going to haunt you forever because it is always going to be there? Or is it only present during specific instances, one time or a few times? In short, is the cause *local or global*? When considering the humiliating experience of solving a set of math problems in its entirety erroneously in front of a class, we can see the cause was most likely because my colleague had had a fight that morning with his wife, and hence, his attention to teaching was not focused and optimal. Is this cause likely universal or pervasive? Most likely not, because the fight was not a universal event. Further, the teacher would be more likely to note that during such fights, he will now the time to decompress and refocus his thoughts before teaching in the future.
2. P_2—**Permanence**: Is the cause likely to change across time, or is it permanent? Is it stable or unstable? Will life remain at the "down" phase forever, or is it possible that the situation will change for the better? Will the principal trying to observe a lesson (one time) forever think that the teacher is ineffective, despite evidence that suggests the contrary? Will the colleague who gave a lackluster presentation in front of high-ranking district officials be forever noted as highly incapable and unknowledgeable, when she was, in fact, the teacher of the year two years before? Will she forever be embarrassed by this unpleasant event, and will her colleagues forever think of her as a failure? Clearly, if these individuals would have just taken a step back and thought about the situation logically, data from the past would suggest they have a better record of solving problems or presenting information to colleagues than bungling them. And

if they had been armed with this knowledge before, they would not have spent so much time stressing about imagined catastrophes happening as a consequence of what had taken place.
3. **P3—Personalization**: Is the cause of the event internal (an attribute that is inherent in the individual) or external (outside of the individual)? Did the event happen because of a defect in the teacher's character? Is it because of a facet of a teacher's personality trait? Or is the cause totally outside or external to and apart from the person? In the previous examples, did the event take place because the math teacher is naturally ditzy, does not know his math, or is disorganized or unfocused? In reality, if he had asked his friends and colleagues, they would have told him that the event did not take place because of a fault in his character or because he had suddenly dropped a significant number of IQ points, rendering him incapable of solving a set of eighth-grade math problems. The cause is external, not internal.

One questionnaire used to evaluate a person's explanatory style is called the ASQ (Attributional Style Questionnaire). It was developed by a team of psychologists, including Seligman, in 1982. In this scale, respondents are presented with hypothetical scenarios and asked to determine the cause if the actual situation had happened. One example is this: "You cannot complete all the tasks assigned to you." (*Does this not describe teaching every day?*) A version of the test (of unknown psychometric properties) has forty-seven items, and it contains a sample statement that reads: "Whatever plans you make, there is always something unexpected that will interfere with them." You can access this test (and take it) at https://testyourself.psychtests.com/. Your response is then scored through seven scales that map to the three dimensions, or three *P*s.

OPTIMISTIC VERSUS PESSIMISTIC EXPLANATORY STYLE

As explained in the first section, there are two ways of thinking in which individuals engage to process the causes of life's ups and downs. These two styles of rationalization are pessimistic and optimistic. A pessimistic style attributes causes of negative events as global, stable, and internal. An optimistic style describes these causes as local, unstable, and external.

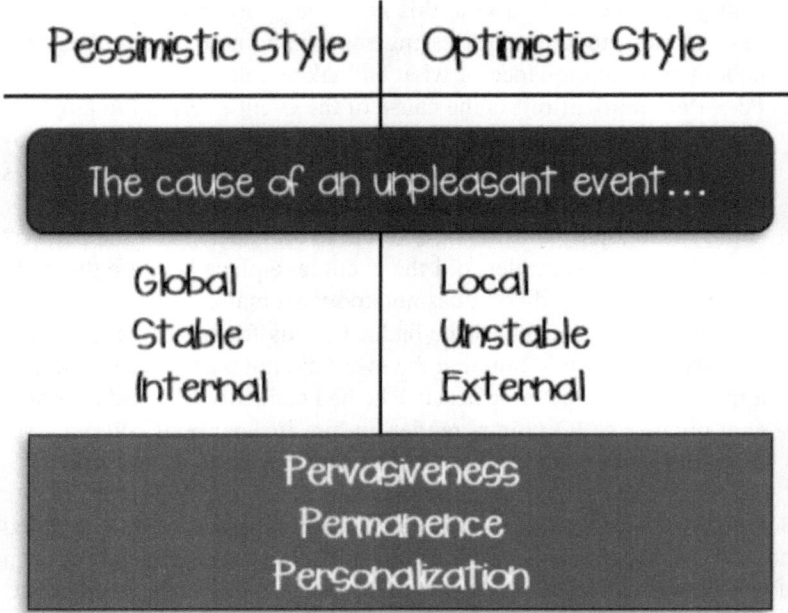

Figure 3.3. Author created.

If a lesson goes wrong, an individual with a pessimistic explanatory style will likely attribute the cause of this event as due to factors that are stable (... *I have always given ineffective lessons, and it will always be this way!*), global (*None of my instructional deliveries are effective or engaging . . .*), and personal or internal (*I was just not born to be a great teacher . . .*). An optimist will rationalize the undesirable event in a different way: with the cause being local (*limited to just this situation*), unstable (*it will not always be this way over time: e.g., Period 2 tomorrow will be better*), and external (*that exceedingly long public announcement threw me off, and I found it difficult to concentrate; I will not allow it to affect me this way again*). Notice that how someone moves forward from the event is influenced by the attribution, as well as how they cope with the negative emotional aftermath.

The surprising thing about explanatory styles is that when good (desirable) events occur, the manner of explaining via the three *P*s gets flipped. A pessimistic style will attribute the cause of such an event as local, unstable, and external (which allows the pessimist to brush

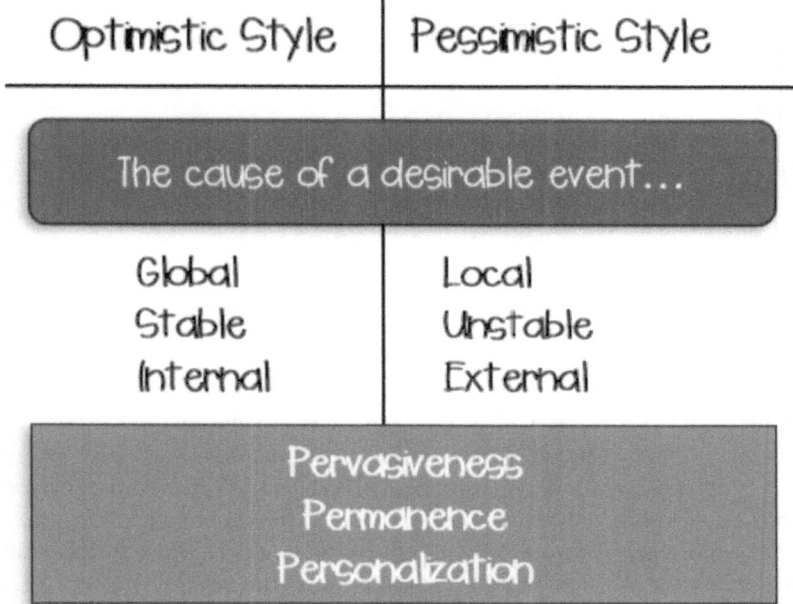

Figure 3.4. Author created.

off any compliments about their knowledge and skills or talents). The optimist will happily explain the cause as global, stable, and internal (*yes, I had something to do with that!*). Hence, when a teacher delivers a highly effective lesson, the individual with the pessimistic explanatory style will consider the event as a once-in-a-lifetime occurrence (*I got lucky!*), as most likely not happening again (unstable), and as due to external factors (*Mr. X helped me write the lesson*, or *the students were exceptionally motivated that day*, or *the PA system did not deliver a terribly long announcement*).

Someone with an optimistic explanatory style will happily explain the cause as global, stable, and internal. Hence, this person can easily move on and respond to any event with an action-focused attitude, without being gripped with helplessness. It is also noticeable that those who have an optimistic explanatory style can happily accept compliments (some people have a challenging time with this) because the attribution is personal (*I worked hard on that presentation and hence, it was a success!*).

How will you explain the following events? Use the three *P*s.

1. *More than half your students failed the math test.*
2. *Your conference with a parent was quite unpleasant. The meeting did not end well.*
3. *The science demonstration did not work, and the students were disappointed.*

ADVANTAGES TO POSSESSING AN OPTIMISTIC EXPLANATORY STYLE

A pessimistic explanatory style leads to such negative emotions as shame, anxiety, and fear. If the cause of a bad event is oneself, then oneself is to blame. And since one's character is the acknowledged cause, then unpleasant events will most likely continue as one's character is considered to be stable, in general. There is hopelessness in the situation, and a tendency to disengage in one's effort. Hence, a pessimistic learning style can constitute a vicious cycle: Bad events lead to self-blame, then an expectancy of future occurrences that will be similarly unpleasant, and a knowledge that no amount of effort will ever lead to a successful future outcome. Consequently, inaction (sometimes paralysis) occurs, and if the problem could have been solved, the inaction will not yield a resolution—and the negative future outcome is almost guaranteed. What a gloomy cycle!

Some scientific studies indicate that such pessimistic explanatory styles are associated with chronic stress, illness, decreased motivation, and depressive thoughts (read more at www.PositivePsychology.com). Those who possess this style of thinking have been shown to spend more days hospitalized, face higher risks for serious health issues, and live shorter lives. Hence, it is advantageous for one's own health (especially educators, who already lead highly stressful lives) to develop an optimistic explanatory style. Students can also benefit from adopting such a mindset. From the positive psychology website, the following benefits were noted:

Figure 3.5. Author created.

- Students who possess an optimistic explanatory style manifest decreased suicidal ideations, compared to those with a pessimistic explanatory style.
- An optimistic explanatory style is positively associated with higher academic performance (*and who would not want that?*). This style was even shown to be predictive of college performance.
- Children with an optimistic explanatory style manifested greater levels of grit, or resilience. They were found to be more likely to persevere through challenges.
- The optimistic explanatory style is also associated with increased job productivity and retention. This is significant in education, as

we know that more than half of new teachers leave during their first five years.
- An optimistic explanatory style has been shown to predict sports performance. Team members with this style manifested greater levels of grit, bouncing back more easily from a loss than those with a pessimistic style. Additionally, players who possess an optimistic explanatory style performed the same, if not better, after negative feedback. The result is the opposite for players with a pessimistic explanatory style.

If all these are outcomes we can achieve from possessing an optimistic explanatory style, there is a solid rationale for teaching and learning it. But it starts with you, the educator: You must develop this way of thinking first before you can model it for your students and colleagues. It also will make you more competent to teach it!

Strategies for Developing an Optimistic Explanatory Style

These are some strategies (adapted from www.PositivePsychology.com) educators can use to develop an optimistic explanatory style:

1. Question your thoughts when you are faced with a negative situation. Enumerate several reasons for why such an event might have happened. (It helps to list these postulated causes on a piece of paper.) While going through this list, identify which causes cannot be solely attributed to you (depersonalize), and identify which causes are external and hence, beyond your control.
2. Whenever you reflect on a negative experience, identify how your current life was influenced by this experience, if at all. Which parts of your current reality were unaffected and remained stable? The goal for this exercise is to ensure that your brain is focused on the actual impact of the negative experience, which most often is negligible. In the example provided about my math colleague, when he looked back at the horrendous mistake of solving math problems wrongly in front of highly attentive middle-school students, the overall impact was insignificant. In fact, the teacher admitted that the event made him more focused and attentive when delivering lessons after that experience. (And he discovered that allowing his

students more "say" in how he demonstrated problem-solving was a better strategy.) He also learned that his students did not respect him any less—in fact, the event became the source of a joke and a lesson about laughing at one's mistakes and moving forward!
3. Practice daily positive affirmations about yourself. Every morning, a friend engages in this wonderful practice: When she first looks in the mirror after awakening, she declares to her reflection positive things that are true about herself. These do not need to include "award-winning" personality attributes. She simply says things that she feels (and knows) are true: *"I am kind. I am empathetic. I am passionate about education. I am a good teacher."* She reflects on how these attributes have remained stable and unaffected by her life's "down" episodes. Just as was previously suggested—to incorporate a "reflection" time at the end of the workday—I would also encourage you to start each day by carving out time in the morning for a routine that involves giving yourself positive affirmations. Don't know how to do it? Check out this little girl on YouTube: https://www.youtube.com/watch?v=kft49ciiHPk.
4. Find a network of people whom you can trust to provide you with an unbiased and objective opinion about your negative experiences. This is not the time to seek the counsel of pessimistic Debbie Downers. Every time a negative event occurs and you are indulging in your rationalization utilizing a pessimistic explanatory style, a friend or two who can provide more objective feedback is a blessing (maybe even more of a necessity!). Having a network of friends who know your strengths and can help you reframe situations in a rational manner will help you to combat the pessimistic attributions. They can also help you cope via action-oriented strategies.

LEARNING OPTIMISM FOR TEACHERS

According to Martin Seligman, optimism can be learned, but it requires effort. A healthy dose of increased awareness and deliberate practice to build the habit of optimism are essential. Because the pessimistic and optimistic learning styles lie on a continuum, an excessive optimistic attributional style can also yield undesirable effects. Some students have shown that individuals who go overboard with a "local-unstable-external" explanatory style for undesirable events can ultimately hold unrealistic perceptions of invincibility. Those with overly optimistic explanatory styles may develop exaggerated self-concepts that are unrealistic. Moreover, an exaggerated optimistic explanatory style can lead an individual to perceive risks as nonconsequential, which then delays the engagement of effective coping skills and results in lowered performance. Therefore, it all goes back to building rational, realistic optimistic explanatory styles.

YOU FEEL AND THEN YOU THINK . . . YOU THINK, THEN YOU FEEL

Thoughts and beliefs play a significant part in the pessimism–optimism explanatory style/construct continuum. Psychologists believe in the power of perceptions and thoughts, as thoughts lead to feelings, which then influence thoughts, which consequently impact feelings—it is a cycle! There is a third spoke in this thinking-feeling wheel, and that is action—whether that behavior is overt or covert. This wheel or cycle is called the cognitive triangle.

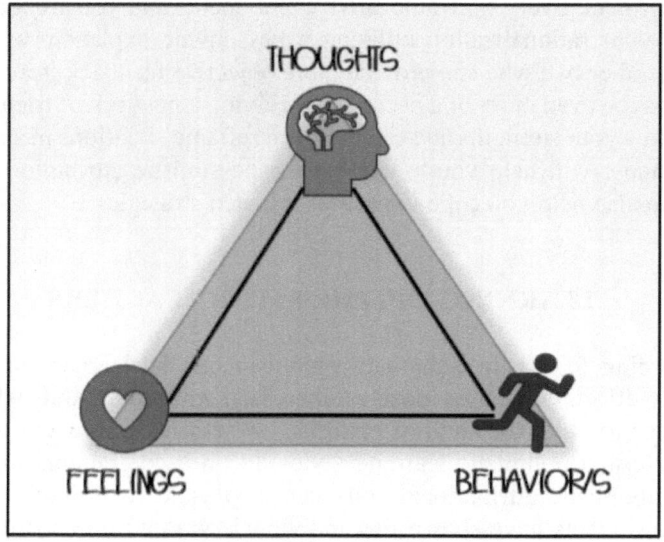

Figure 3.6. The Cognitive Triangle. Author created.

This cognitive triangle forms the foundaticn of cognitive behavior therapy. If an individual can arrest their undesirable and ineffective thinking processes, then he or she can influence his or her emotions and subsequent actions. Imagine a student who is about to take a test. She thinks she will do well because she has studied, and she can look back at past experiences of test-taking to note that she has (in most of these occasions) performed well. These thoughts influence her attitude and feelings toward test-taking. She comes to the testing room feeling confident—maybe a little nervous, but optimistic that she will do well. She is also motivated to do her best. Hence, her focus and attention are not hampered, and her desire to perform well is not adversely affected by negative thoughts.

Too often, teachers try to employ shorthanded strategies to boost confidence in test-taking by speaking the following ineffective, shallow declarations to their classes that, most likely, will not lead to the desired outcomes:

"You will all do well in this test."
"This test is easy!"
"Just read the directions carefully."

Why are these attempts described as "ineffective"? Are these not inspirational and motivating statements to share? While such declarations are well-intentioned, they do not get at the root of the cognitive triangle. They influence thoughts, not on the day of the test, but maybe weeks before. How does this sound shortly before the day of the test? *"We have prepared for this test. We have discussed the concepts thoroughly, and all of you have had sufficient time to review the material. We have looked at the structure of the test, and we have practiced taking a similar test."* Followed by: *"Do you have any reasons for thinking that you may fail the test?"* (Of course, this processing is not done during the exact day of the exam).

These are opportunities we need to provide our students with consistent times to process pessimistic thinking, question their thoughts, and discuss possible courses of action before the test that can lead to more positive outcomes. The good news is that the cycle is reinforcing (although this could be bad news, too!). If positive thoughts lead to pleasant feelings, which lead to open-mindedness and the exploration of more effective actions, then the behavior resulting from this will reinforce the positive thoughts and pleasant feelings. But also think of the opposite: Negative thoughts lead to unpleasant feelings, which then lead to an incapacity to act or engage in problem-solving actions. The problem or issue will then remain unresolved, leading to the same cycle of unpleasant thoughts, feelings, and a lack of effective action.

Chapter Four

Cycle of Fear and Learned Helplessness

THE FEAR CYCLE AND A LOSS OF HOPE

Negative emotions, such as sadness, shame, and guilt, have acquired a bad reputation. These emotions are, indeed, unpleasant—think of guilt, shame, sadness, envy, disgust, and fear. These emotions can cause an individual to be miserable and may make people dislike themselves and others, as well as decrease confidence, self-efficacy, and self-esteem. People who experience negative emotions may propel their miserable state of mind and project it onto others. It is not difficult to predict the association of negative emotions with the erosion of job satisfaction and goal motivation.

In the world of education and school, with the added stress inherent in the job of teaching or being an administrator accountable for the effective functioning of schools, negative emotions can easily become widespread due to "emotion contagion." Emotion contagion occurs when an emotion appears to spread via osmosis; it appears when people who observe the emotions and behaviors of another assimilate and externalize those same emotions and behaviors.

Have you ever been cheerful all morning, but then experienced feeling grumpy after spending twenty minutes in the faculty lounge? While acknowledging that not all faculty rooms across schools are universal centers for griping and complaining (not that venting is not good for the soul sometimes), we also must realize that within these spaces, emotion contagion appears to take place—and spread. Consequently, some educators may consider these areas as mental health "danger" zones and may avoid visiting them. One teacher stated feeling drained and fatigued after each visit. Some teachers recounted experiencing continuous blame and venting; by itself, this is not necessarily a "bad" thing, but the discussions are usually not geared toward finding solutions, which can be frustrating. Hence, the faculty room can be known as a fermentation vat for negative emotions.

However, as stated before, negative emotions have a place in our mental health repertoire. Experiencing these emotions will intensify the feeling of the positive emotions when they occur. Joy is much more pleasant, sweeter, and welcome when experienced after sadness. Negative emotions can also serve as warning systems: Think of anger and how it propels us to act. Like positive emotions, our negative emotions are survival mechanisms; they send signals to our brains, cautioning us to be extra-vigilant. Think of your sense of disgust after eating something bad; that may be a signal that we should not be partaking of whatever it is that elicited that response. Negative emotions tell our bodies and brains that our survival and well-being may be threatened.

QUESTION: *What are the top-five negative emotions?*
ANSWER: *Anger, fear, resentment, frustration, and anxiety*
QUESTION: *Which emotions are most commonly experienced by students and teachers every day?*
ANSWER: *Anger, fear, resentment, frustration, and anxiety*

It is quite easy to imagine how these negative emotions can be triggered. For a student, it could be anger at oneself for being late to class, fear of making a bad quiz score, resentment at the vice principal for "picking" on him/her, frustration at not understanding the day's chemistry lesson, and anxiety over a forthcoming final examination. A teacher might also go through this roller coaster of negative emotions in a single day, experiencing anger at the PA system that suddenly blares an announcement when she is in the middle of teaching, fear concerning an upcoming administrator visit for an evaluation, resentment at having to cover for another teacher's bus duty (for the third time this week), frustration at students not "getting" the lesson despite two days of extra reteaching, and anxiety over forthcoming state assessments. These negative emotions can make the life of the teacher (or the student) quite stressful.

THE KING OF NEGATIVE EMOTIONS: FEAR

It can be argued that fear is the most unpleasant of all emotions. It is powerful and natural. Fear is an "alert signal," causing us to be aware of a danger potential, or threat of harm. It is an emotional response to a perceived danger that can be either physical or psychological. Fear is discussed in this chapter in relation to risk avoidance and learned helplessness. When we have a crippling fear of failure, we may resort to avoidance efforts as a coping strategy. This not only happens among students, but it also occurs among adults.

- Reflection Questions: *How can fear result in risk avoidance? How could risk avoidance be harmful?*

Fear varies in intensity across a spectrum. Paul Ekman (2021), a well-known psychologist with expertise in the study of emotions, describes an escalating intensity of fear, ranging from trepidation, to nervousness, anxiety, dread, desperation, panic, and horror, all the way to terror. Fear also occurs in a cycle (see figure 4.1 below), as explained/adapted from the Lisa Lam Coaching website (2021):

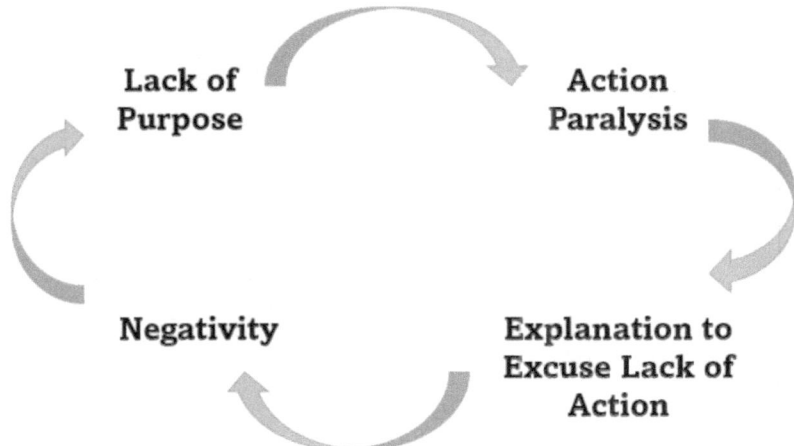

Figure 4.1. Author created.

This diagram can be unpacked and subsequently applied to various teaching and learning scenarios. An individual may start feeling a loss of purpose or meaning in the work she or he does. This leads to paralysis, in which the individual freezes and avoids taking action for fear of failure, or even as the result of a lack of motivation. This inaction leads to excuses, as the person attempts to reconcile why other individuals are successful and happy. Rationalization happens at this stage, where others' successes are explained as due to luck or being at the right place at the right time. Finally, negativity ensues.

The lack of progress, the continued realization that others are achieving success, and the challenges of finding a rationale for these successes ultimately take a toll, resulting in a cascade of negativity within the individual's mind. This includes a cacophony of negative emotions, such as frustration, sadness, shame, and guilt. This subsequently fuels a feeling of lack of purpose, and the cycle starts again. The fear cycle is a considerable barrier to optimism.

Lacking purpose, being paralyzed such that no action is taken, coming up short when comparisons with others are made, and experiencing a torrent of negative emotions—e.g., guilt, shame, sadness, anxiety, and frustration—lead to a mental state in which hope and optimism cannot take root. And because it is a cycle, escaping from any of the four phases may prove challenging. Have you ever been gripped in this cycle of fear? In the world of education, the fear of failure, or even just not living up to preconceived expectations, is perhaps the most pernicious fear there is. Let us look at two examples:

Table 4.1.

	Teacher	Student
Bad Event:	While being observed, Mrs. X delivers a "bad" lesson. Students were not engaged, and the lesson fell flat.	Student Y receives a second failing exam score in Chemistry.
Paralysis	The failed lesson causes Mrs. X to avoid being creative in future lesson planning, for fear of failing again. She sticks to canned lesson plans in the effort to "stay safe."	Student Y internalizes that no amount of effort will bring success (more about this condition will be explained later!). S/he decides to do nothing for fear of failing more abominably.

	Teacher	Student
Excuses	Mrs. X hears about the successes of other teachers in her department. She makes excuses about her "failure" and others' success as a coping strategy: "They must be the principal's favorites!"	Student Y sees and hears how other students in his/her chemistry class are getting high scores. S/he begins rationalizing these performances: "They must be the teacher's favorites."
Negativity	Negative emotions cascade forward: shame, guilt, frustration, disgust, and fear concerning the next observation.	Negative emotions cascade forward: shame, guilt, frustration, disgust, and fear concerning the next observation.
Purposelessness	What she once thought as the "best" job on the planet begins to lack meaning. S/he wonders whether she should stick it out.	What s/he once thought as a most enjoyable subject, and a promising major in college, begins to seem unappealing.

LEARNED HELPLESSNESS: WHEN FAILURE BECOMES NORMAL (AND EXPECTED) IN THE MIND

A psychological condition called learned helplessness is related to being in the grip of the fear cycle and not seeming able to escape. Learned helplessness results when an individual finally gives up after repeated experiences with failure. The internalized message is that no amount or quality of effort or help can lead to success, so why even bother trying? A remarkable feature of learned helplessness is the disengagement from effort, even if that effort is clearly within reach and when success is apparent.

Remember the student who refuses even to write his name on a piece of paper that you already supplied? Or the student who does not even want to pick up her pen despite repeated promptings? Or the student who will engage in avoidant behaviors that require more energy to avoid reading a paragraph than just reading the paragraph would expend? Remember the student who declared fiercely and repeatedly that *"you can't make me do anything!"*? They may be students in the grip of learned helplessness! Adults can also suffer from this condition. Here are some manifestations of learned helplessness:

- Avoidance of risks
- Disengagement from effort
- Lack of motivation
- Helpless resignation to failure
- Refusal to take advantage of help being offered

Astonishingly, learned helplessness can be induced. One YouTube video of a professor shows how giving half her students puzzles that were impossible to solve was enough to make them give up. The students got stuck in the paralysis stage of the fear cycle! Even when the professor at the end gave them all a set of puzzles that were very easy to solve, the students refused to put in the effort. Adults can become stuck in the paralysis stage of the fear cycle, too, and experience helplessness when confronted with a task. Do you have a colleague who refuses to accept any help, insisting that the outcome will be bad regardless? Have you ever been frustrated trying to convince this colleague to try several different strategies, only to be met with the conviction that none of them will work?

There is no convincing the individual who is gripped in learned helplessness! Every suggestion and offer of help will be met with a shake of the head and a resigned sigh. This was exactly a fellow administrator's experience when trying to mentor a new teacher ("new," meaning she came from a different professional field) about classroom management. No strategy would work, according to her way of thinking, because the students would misbehave anyway, or the parents would be accusatory and unengaged anyway. It was very frustrating for the administrator to try to get the teacher the help she needed, as she refused anything and everyone who tried to assist her! In the following pages, two stories will be recounted about learned helplessness, based on the author's experiences.

LEARNED HELPLESSNESS STORY 1: JESSICA R, THE SEVENTH-GRADE REPEATER

Jessica M was a high school student in a posh private school in the Philippines. (Only 1 percent of the population would likely be able to attend this particular school.) She was a student in a colleague's Integrated Science I class, but she needed help in math. Her teachers described her as the most easily distracted student in the school. Her mother, a renowned defense lawyer in the Philippines, was going out of her wits trying to find help for Jessica. A fellow teacher decided to tutor her in math, as she was already repeating her high school freshman year.

Jessica proved to be a great challenge! She was the poster child for learned helplessness (although no one at school was aware of this condition at that time). She had failed almost every subject during her freshman year in high school, and she had subsequently disengaged from any form of schoolwork. She had been asked to repeat the seventh grade (in the Philippines at that time, "high school" began in the seventh grade). Per her tutor's recounting, she wouldn't even pick up a pen, except to practice twirling it. She could not write out an equation with the equal sign in its proper place; she could not even write the whole equation out straight on lined paper, as it would always appear skewed and sloping downward. She could not stay focused for even ten minutes. Her pencil always needed sharpening. She consistently lost her calculator. She was always getting hungry. She couldn't locate her notebook. However, she could become so hyper-focused on having perfect handwriting that her paper would literally disintegrate from her incessant erasing. The tutor tried many strategies to motivate and inspire her to listen and put more effort into the math, but it was a daily battle for her to complete even the most mundane academic tasks.

Fortunately, the tutor was quite patient and decided to take things slowly, in incremental "baby" steps. Together, they wrote out super-simple equations (that is, the tutor wrote them very slowly, and the student watched and listened). The tutor made it fun by having the student write out some equations in the air, using her fingers to gesture the numbers and variables. She drew a square every time Jessica wrote an equation, so she would know where the "equal" sign belonged (and sometimes this was all she did—write the equal sign correctly). The sessions were long because they had to stop every few minutes. The tutor and Jessica went back several grade levels to build the requisite foundations. They used cardstock paper so she could erase without causing a hole to form on the paper. It took months before she learned that perfection could be overrated. They celebrated every success, no matter how small. When Jessica first learned how to write an equation all lined up, without needing a box for the equal sign, the whole family whooped with joy!

Jessica finished that year a resounding success. Her teachers were all happily surprised that she not only passed Algebra, but she even received a B. The year she took to repeat a grade was also the year she needed to overcome learned helplessness, break out of the fear cycle, and regain her confidence and hope. Note that this is not an endorsement for grade retention. It just happened to work for Jessica as she needed the extra time.

LEARNED HELPLESSNESS STORY 2: MRS. AK, THE DISBELIEVING TEACHER

Unlike the first scenario, this account is not a success story. A friend and fellow immigrant (Mrs. MP) from the Philippines had a very tough first year of teaching in the United States. One might argue that the first five years were all tough for her, but it was during her second year that she sought out social support and relationships with peers to help mitigate the stress of teaching and acclimating to a new country, particularly in a Title I (high-poverty) school. During these socialization efforts, she met AK, an English teacher. Teaching was AK's third career, having transitioned from a job in business and sales. Because they both taught the same group of students in junior high, the two teachers frequently met and collaborated.

However, instead of making Mrs. MP feel more confident and effective at her new teaching job, the interactions with AK always left her drained instead. Mrs. MP was a "new" teacher in the United States, trying to fit in and belong, but also regain her success. (She had been a successful teacher in the Philippines.) However, connecting with AK soon became an added stressor in her life. AK was always caught up in some kind of drama, in which the situation was quite pitiful and difficult. She was the star of one failed dramatic event after another: bad observations, misbehaving students, disrespectful parents, demanding grandmothers, incompetent site leaders, and uncooperative counselors, to name a few. Each problem AK recounted (from failed lessons to contentious meetings with parents) presented opportunities for MK to help by making suggestions.

However, AK would declare all recommendations untenable, doomed to fail, and consequently, not worth a try. MP even ended up creating lesson plans for her, as well as behavior plans for her challenging students, and she spent time finding resources that AK never used, and she covered for her sixth period (during her prep) because AK could not "deal" with the misbehaving kids. (All kids are misbehaving, by the way!) AK refused to believe that "those" kids actually were model students in the other classrooms, including an honors science class. She refused to do observations and attend professional development.

AK was an adult in the grip of learned helplessness, and unfortunately, she drew everyone with whom she interacted into her circle of gloom and doom. She was ultimately paired with a mentor teacher, but that team was not successful, either. AK was eventually transferred to a different school at the end of the year, and finally her contract was not renewed. Understanding what we now know about learned helplessness, perhaps more could have been done to help AK.

ADDRESSING LEARNED HELPLESSNESS

Learned helplessness is challenging to address as it is quite well established in childhood, before the student even gets to school. However, some ideas may help mitigate the "symptoms." Here are a few of them:

- **Examine your grading practices:** Do you believe that handing out zeros motivates students? If so, it may be time to rethink that practice. No student has ever been motivated by a zero. Another policy to examine is that of not allowing redos or retakes. Not allowing the opportunity to try again may be sending the message that a failure is final and permanent. If educators can retake their credential exams, and are able to exercise "do-overs" for projects at work or lesson plans that fell flat, don't our students deserve similar grace?

- **Normalize and celebrate failure:** Have you ever tried "My Favorite No" as a strategy? Google it on YouTube! This approach teaches that without failure, we don't learn. Teachers can also model how to appropriately respond to failure and share stories of famous scientists and inventors who successfully reframed failure as an opportunity to learn and discover. The stories of Marie Curie, Thomas Edison, and fifteen-year-old Jake Andraka are useful narratives about the value of failure and resilience.
- **Praise and encourage the effort, not the perceived intrinsic ability of the student:** Say, "*I can tell how much effort that took—congratulations!*" instead of "*You're really brilliant at math.*" This is important because it reframes success as the result of effort, not because of an already-existing, intrinsic ability. As educators, we need to consistently examine our language. Hang posters in your room that emphasize effort over perceived ability, and reference them constantly when teaching and providing feedback. Another strategy is to place stickie notes around your workspace with reminders like these: "Emphasize effort"; "Praise diligence"; and "Normalize failure!" You could also post more appropriate feedback that emphasizes effort in visible places in your classroom.
- **Model an optimistic mindset:** Grab every opportunity to show that academic failure isn't personal, pervasive, or permanent. Failure isn't forever! Model how to appropriately cope with failure by using it as a launch-off point for learning. Have you ever caught yourself teaching something erroneous or making a mistake? Well, what a great opportunity to recognize the error, perhaps laugh at it, and celebrate it by declaring, "Now that we know what method does *not* work, let's explore more effective ones!"
- **Work with students to set bite-sized goals and celebrate in a big way when they achieve them:** With a big project, have a checklist that empowers students to start small and observe their progress at each step. Provide a collection of accessible resources (e.g., a visual dictionary, caring adults, websites, a peer coach) for students as they are working on their goals. In short, chunk the pathway to success.

The real antidote to learned helplessness is learned optimism—of the realistic kind. Model and teach it to students, family members, and friends. Several strategies have already been shared: positive reframing, arresting negative self-talk, exercising selective focusing, using humor, and avoiding catastrophizing. Another way to address learned helplessness is to teach students how to think about events in a positive light—yes, you guessed it! Teach them how to think with a positive explanatory style!

SELF-REFLECTION QUESTIONS

- Have you ever experienced being gripped with feelings of helplessness? Think about how you dealt with those intense feelings.
- Do you know of anyone who seems to be currently gripped by learned helplessness? How do you interact with this person?

Chapter Five

Realistic Optimism, Hope, Decompression, and Emotional Detachment

Today was the day they announced a new variant: *Omicron!* You will perhaps agree that this is such an ominous-sounding name—especially for a cousin (or perhaps a brother or sister?) of the SARS-COVID-2 virus that killed more than a million people in the United States alone. We can easily conjure the image of an evil ball of a virus with at least (as they currently described) ten mutations that have made it far more sinister because of their very high rates of infectivity. In the midst of all the gloom and doom concerning this news, there are those "realistic optimists" who refuse to curl up in a ball and cry—although the urge must really be great! For this author, the greatest challenge during the pandemic had been waiting to be able to go back home (if her home country ever opened its borders) to visit her family more than six thousand miles away (last seen in 2019)—and now this news killed every ounce of optimism the author possessed.

It was quite challenging to summon and foster hope when we were surrounded with negativity about this recent turn of events everywhere we turned. The news and social media coverage appeared to dish out gloom and doom—sickness, death, destruction, inflation, protests against masks and vaccinations, and overall chaos. Yet, hope was sorely needed! Throughout the constant trials and tribulations of life, hope is definitely an effective coping strategy. Despite what you might hear from educational experts who seem to dismiss the importance of hope, we can argue that persons must first possess hope because *hope is essential!* Being hopeless makes all other strategies untenable and

> **QUESTIONS TO PONDER**
>
> 1. How is hope NOT a strategy in the context of teaching and learning?
>
> 2. Why would education experts *not* advocate for hope?
>
> 3. As a teacher, how does hope play a role in the important work that you do?
>
> 4. As a learner, how is hope important?

Figure 5.1. Author created.

not worth trying. To those who say that hope is never a good plan, it can be countered that we cannot even develop a plan—or *conceive* of a plan—much less implement that plan, if we don't possess any hope to start with. *Hope is a strategy!* Hope is the *first* strategy. Hope is the *only* strategy! Everything must start with hope (*and its broader construct, optimism*).

REALISTIC OPTIMISM, ANYONE?

When a person is convinced that a future outcome could be successful, that person is optimistic. However, optimism (and its cousin, pessimism) occurs on a gradient, as discussed in chapter 1. Along this gradient resides a brand of optimism that is excessive and can be harmful: unrealistic optimism, which can lead to toxic positivity. This scale, revisited (see Figure 5.2), has realistic pessimism and unrealistic pessimism as part of the spectrum:

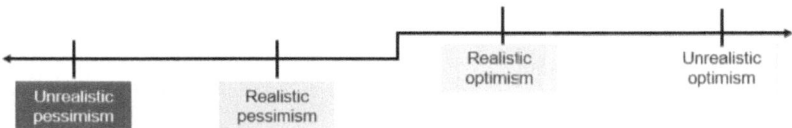

Figure 5.2. The Pessimism/Optimism Scale. Author created.

This scale is purposefully not straight (see that climb up in the middle?)—this is because having a more optimistic worldview, or mindset, takes work, or effort: *It is a climb up!* In any organization, it is quite easy to spot those who perpetually reside in the farthest left and farthest right sides of the spectrum. They are the ones whom we tend to avoid, those who suck all joy from our souls in a minute of interaction, leaving us feeling drained, exhausted, and unhappy. These are the unrealistic pessimists. It does not matter what the situation, condition, or circumstances are; these people have the ability to leap into the most catastrophic predictions in a single bound. The ones on the far right are also not helpful, as they always paint an unrealistically rosy picture of events. They abound in an excessive and unsupported view of a happy and optimistic outcome across all contexts. This overgeneralization of happy events coming to fruition at all times results in denial of reality, a minimization of risks, and ultimately the invalidation of the "realness" of difficult situations in the lives of other people.

Review the table below and consider a particular person or individuals in your workplace or family who exhibits such a mindset.

Table 5.1. The Unrealistic Pessimist in Hypothetical Classroom Scenarios

Bad News	Good News
"Funding for XYZ has been cut." • *Well, that is it! We will most likely lose our jobs.*	"Funding for XYZ is increased this year!" • *Well, money does not come free. This probably means more work for us . . . and we had better not rely on this money to be here next year . . ."*
"Our test scores have dropped significantly these last two years." • *Our enrollment will most likely drop! Who wants to enroll their child in an inferior school? We may have to close in five years... or less!*	"Our test scores have significantly improved this year! Great work, everyone!" • *This is most likely a fluke. There is no reason to expect that our achievement will remain this high!*
"Mold has been detected in Room 508. We need to move some classrooms around . . ." • *Does this mean we will all get sick? I can't get sick! This will affect my retirement!*	"The inspection indicated no mold. So, we do not need to move classrooms around." • *Those inspectors are mistaken. Wait another year, and they will tell us there is definitely mold in these old buildings. Just wait until someone gets really, really sick!*

Some of the reactions described in the table probably caused you to laugh and think of a certain friend, family member, or coworker. One fellow teacher (Miss M), who was new to her school, recounted the following story. As a new faculty member, she befriended a fellow English teacher, and both of them made a habit of sitting together at events (lunch, assemblies, faculty meetings, workshops). Such a practice made the event more bearable, particularly if it was mandated. Other staff members even joked that she (Miss M) had a workplace spouse: Mrs P.

Everything was great that first year. Except soon, Miss M noticed that during staff meetings, every time the principal announced a piece of news, whether good or bad, Mrs. P would whisper that a catastrophic outcome was to be expected based on the news! Mrs. P was quite gifted at conjuring up the most unpleasant future consequences or outcomes! Miss M tried to explain that cancellation of a field trip did not automatically mean the district was in a dire or hopeless financial situation causing teachers to lose their jobs. Her attempts were unsuccessful. She began to realize that her new best friend made her anxious every Wednesday morning.

So, here's a strategy to follow after considering this example: *Do not sit with an unrealistic pessimist during faculty meetings.* This is akin to having a "dire future whisperer" whose effect is to sprinkle gloom and doom in every circumstance. This constant barrage of negative predictions can cause emotional exhaustion in the listener.

But on the other hand, what about the unrealistic optimist, the one brimming with toxic positivity? Although arguably, the effect on the other's demeanor might not be as exhausting or anxiety-inducing, the unrealistic optimist is not a good friend to one's psyche. Here's a table that illustrates how the unrealistic optimist might respond to a few situations:

Table 5.2. The Unrealistic Optimist in Hypothetical School/Classroom Scenarios

Bad News	Good News
"Funding for XYZ has been cut." • That's a bummer! But I am pretty sure we will receive another grant funding! Time to celebrate!	"Funding for XYZ is increased this year!" • And it will continue increasing! We will probably receive double that amount! Let's plan to buy that new, expensive math program!
"Our test scores have dropped significantly these last two years." • Pooh! That is no big deal. Wait for next year, and our scores will be off the charts. I can just feel it!	"Our test scores have significantly improved this year! Great work, everyone!" • I knew this would happen! Just wait for next year—we will be the best school in the region!
"Mold has been detected in Room 508. We need to move some classrooms around . . ." • What? Well, I will most likely land in that big room behind the theater! Help me begin planning for the move, okay? I need help decorating!	"The inspection indicated no mold. So, we do not need to move classrooms around." • These buildings may be old, but there is no reason to suspect mold! There should be no more discussion of this topic for years to come!

Would you rather . . .?

- Spend a weekend with an unrealistic pessimist, or an unrealistic optimist? Why?
- Have a teaching partner who is an unrealistic pessimist or an unrealistic optimist? Why?
- Work for a principal who is an unrealistic pessimist, or an unrealistic optimist? Why?

These scenarios probably elicited a couple of chuckles from you! An unrealistic optimist has the worldview that *nothing can possibly go wrong*, that the future will always be rosy. There is danger in this mindset, as success is not equated with effort in the unrealistic optimist's mind—to them, success just comes and is to be expected. The unrealistic optimist is a superhero, able to *leap into the land of a bright and rosy future in a single bound!* Can you imagine what conversations you might have if you were to sit with such an individual during a faculty meeting? Do you have a friend who has such a worldview? It must be exhausting to listen to so many bright, rosy outcomes if you are dealing with a present context of challenging realities.

Here's another story: A colleague, Mrs. X, once made the mistake of inviting a friend (Mrs. Y) to spend a vacation with her. It was a seven-day cruise, with some days being "locked up" at sea. By the second day, Mrs. X was ready to declare a divorce from her friend. Mrs. X was always happy and loudly exuding positive vibes all day, even when the sea was choppy and most passengers were feeling sick! She was "doling" out positive quotes to everyone on board, solicited or not (mostly not). She was also in the habit of shaming or chastising others for expressing authentic feelings that were not up to her standard of unbridled positivity. The seven-day cruise turned out to be, sadly, the end of Mrs. X and Mrs. Y's friendship.

The unrealistic optimist will also drain your energy as it forces an internal struggle within your mind to counter his or her worldview with a more realistic picture. It becomes not only challenging, but also exhausting to "keep up" with this internal struggle and constantly remind yourself of the cognitive dissonance between what you know of the reality as opposed to what you are constantly hearing from the unrealistic optimist. Unfortunately, spending time with an unrealistic optimist will not make an individual happier or more hopeful. The opposite outcome is much more likely.

TOXIC POSITIVITY MOVES

Do you know of individuals who . . .

- Dismiss others' emotions, saying, "Just smile, everything will be okay!"?
- Make you feel guilty for feeling less than brimming with positivity ("You need to just laugh it off!")?
- Shame or chastise you whenever you express frustration or dissatisfaction?
- Offer unhelpful positive advice that is empty and ineffective?
- Say, "It could be worse!" when you are unloading your authentic feelings?

THE ART AND SCIENCE OF DECOMPRESSION AND DETACHMENT

Hope, and subsequently optimism, requires that educators (and others who are in service-oriented fields) develop an awareness of and mastery of two skill sets. These are the twin skills of decompression and detachment. Teaching (or being an educator, or even working in the healthcare field) is an overly stressful occupation. Someone once described it as a day filled with a thousand decisions to be made, or constantly operating a brain (one's own) with hundreds of browser tabs open and running. It is not only stressful, but exhausting—physically and emotionally. It is one of the few jobs in which the employee cannot just use the restroom when he or she needs to: A teacher has *to plan a trip* to the restroom during his or her prep: *Your bladder must accommodate the class schedule!*

The exhaustion associated with teaching is also significantly daunting as you are always on comprehensive (nonstop) high alert. With thirty to thirty-five students to care for, there is no time to "un-switch" during the school day; that is, there is no downtime. A teacher is always on the lookout for behaviors (and environmental cues) that can derail the teaching and learning cycle. At the end of the day, your brain (and your whole body) doesn't just "turn off" at will. An educator cannot just command his or her body and mind to shut off like a switch. There is significant effort required to release all the stresses of the day. You must also consider that, unlike other professions, a workday for a teacher usually involves very minimal social interaction with other adults—or none at all. Physical and emotional exhaustion becomes a daily challenge. Because of this, educators must design and plan a decompression routine. Your job satisfaction and longevity in the field depends on it. Your students' success also depends on this.

Decompression: The Skill of Slowly Shutting Down the Stresses of the Day

Take a moment and answer the following questions:

- What time does your workday end?
- What time do you, on average, leave school (or your workplace)?
- How long is your commute home?
- When you get home, what chores do you immediately have to do?

Essentially, do you have a "space" between the time when you clock out of work and when you assume your personal role of a wife, mother, or homemaker—or even a dog mommy? Does this "space" include time for you (and a place where you cannot be disturbed) to reflect and let go of the day's stress? You need this space and time as a "decompression" space. You need to create this opportunity, and you need to make it a habit.

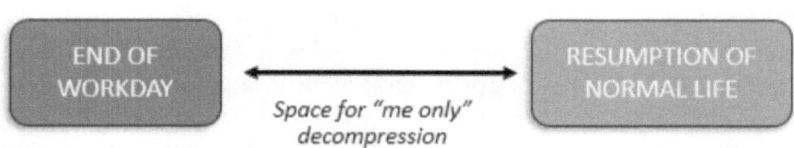

Figure 5.3. Where Decompression Lies. Author created.

Here is a story that illustrates why this decompression time is so needed. In 2014, a close friend accepted the position of an assistant principal to a high-performing high school that required a five-hour drive (*it was a dream job!*). While most individuals would probably consider a five-hour drive to be brutal and even a deal-breaker, it proved to be a blessing to Felicia. Note that Felicia is a housewife, but she has no young children to take care of (although she does have a much-loved dog). She has a husband who just recently lost his job and was able to stay home. It was not until after Felicia left this position that she realized that the two-hour commute to work plus the three hours spent returning home, considering the traffic-infested rush hours on Interstate-80, was a blessing. How did this happen? She had found her decompression zone! Or rather, *it was forced on her!*

In psychology, *decompression* is described as a process whereby an individual attempts to return to a normal, more relaxed state after a period of intense stress, psychological pressure, or frenetic activity. Felicia's drive back home—all three hours of it—afforded her the place and time she needed to decompress, and by the time she got home, she was astonished to find herself more relaxed, less stressed, and fully human again. (And no, she did not do yoga or meditate while driving—she did have calm music playing). She arrived home quite tired, but astonishingly she was also happier and calmer. Additionally, she was more ready to transition to the next phase—detachment—which will be described in the next section.

What happens during a successful decompression period? What opportunities present themselves during this time? And why are these opportunities so important to our mental well-being?

- We need time to process the day—*warts and all, good and bad*—alone, with no one evaluating or judging us.
- We need time for a gratitude check. Felicia forced herself to rehearse *five* good things that had happened during the day (*yes, at least five*). The decompression time provided the opportunity for her to feel and savor the joy again—a time that was denied from her during the busy day. During a busy workday, individuals seldom have the time to truly relish positive emotions or feelings.
- We need time to ask self-reflection questions and engage in some metacognition, including: (1) In what areas could I have provided a

better response? (2) What areas were within my control today? (3) What areas were beyond my control? (4) What could I have done better? What could I resolve to do better in the future?
- We may need to scold ourselves for things done wrong—and brainstorm ways to do better. During this time, within the safety of the car, Felicia was able to answer her questions. She could privately scold herself and engage in brainstorming ideas, again without fear of judgment. She could acknowledge areas for improvement. After the scolding, she could reaffirm that she was a good human being and she had acted with good intentions. She could make a mental checklist of how she could more intelligently deal with the situation if it presented itself again. She could even shout out loud that she had done enough! And Felicia never forgot to give herself a pep talk.

If you do this, be prepared to get strange looks or stares from fellow drivers, as clearly they will be able to see you talking while driving (even gesticulating, when safe to do so) inside the car with no other passengers. What joy to be with oneself, to have the time to process the stresses of the day, to be able to shout when needed! And yes, there will be many times when sobbing is part of the decompression process too. For Felicia, there was comfort in knowing that every workday, the car (her space) and commute back home (her time) was available for decompression.

This time could have been spent eating copious amounts of snacks and drinking jugs of coffee while blaring loud music, but it was more productively used to acknowledge her weaknesses and strengths, as well as process with a clearer mind, the experiences of the day. Most importantly, it was a great time for Felicia to just be able to say, "I love me." Now, when do you get to do that? When do you find the time to affirm yourself? When do you get to tell yourself you have done something good? You praise and affirm your dog many times during the day (*"Such a good boy!"* or *"Good girl!"*), but when did you last spend at least fifteen minutes affirming the fact that you are a good person whose intentions are positive and whose actions are ethical? You need this decompression time because it is also a time for showing love for yourself.

The critical importance of this ability to decompress at the end of each day was realized when a new position presented itself to Felicia, and she gleefully accepted it. Her commute time to work was reduced to a mere seventeen minutes one way! What a joyful blessing (or so it seemed) to not have to drive five hours a day! Although the position was a step above in the education career ladder, and it also provided great opportunities for learning, the loss of Felicia's important decompression time was excruciating for her. It turned out that seventeen minutes was not enough time to reflect and decompress, savor the good things that had happened during the day, do a Q and A with herself, shout, cry, and affirm that she was actually a good, decent human being.

The loss of her decompression opportunity was felt immediately during the first week, and even more so as relationship-building and a much learning was required during her first year of transition. The *space* was present (her little Kia Soul remained), but not the *time*. What happened at the end of each day was unexpected—emotional and physical exhaustion that resulted in feelings of grumpiness and a short fuse. Anxiety and panic attacks came back with a vengeance and occurred intermittently during the night. Incriminating self-doubts and crippling catastrophizing returned.

It is most likely that the inability to decompress sufficiently before returning home was the cause for Felicia's sudden and ongoing distress. During this first year that this decompression opportunity was denied, her happiness dwindled, and even though there were successes to be noted due to great relationships being built and joyful tasks also abounded, the loss of time spent commuting to and from work also led to other unanticipated consequences. This time was also valuable for affirmations, joyful anticipation, and planning her workday. And hence a natural consequence was a new and constant feeling of panic, of being unprepared for the day, and Felicia's confidence in her abilities dwindled.

A surprising event happened to her one day as, instead of adopting the usual seventeen-minute route from the new workplace, she found herself driving toward the bay area (her old workplace), almost on autopilot. Astonishingly, she began to engage in the process of decompressing, and it took five exits for her to realize that she was not on her usual route. She immediately turned back and drove around her neighborhood (five times) to finish her decompression tasks. That trip home ended with a new resolve. If she were to take the longest possible route home, even just twice a week, she could "burn" thirty minutes, which could then be spent decompressing.

Yes, this would mean higher gas costs (perhaps an electric car is in the future for Felicia!). At first it might seem counterintuitive when you think about it, but in reality, an individual, especially an educator, cannot function well as a wife, mother, or just a normal person if they are not mentally well, and decompression can reset you to a better emotional state. So, here's a strategy: Find a way to decompress—alone—with your thoughts at the end (and if possible, also at the start) of each workday. This could mean driving around the neighborhood three times before actually coming home.

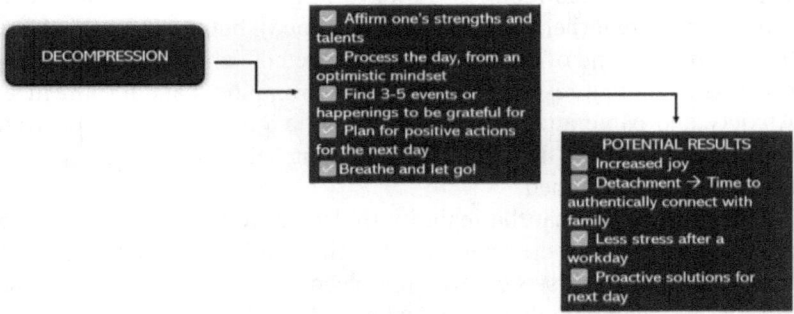

Figure 5.4. The Art of Decompression and Postulated Effects. Author created.

AND NOW DETACHMENT!

Once you have mastered decompression as a habit, the next coping strategy on your way to being hopeful and optimistic is detachment. This is perhaps the most difficult strategy to master and make a routine or a habit. As educators, it is very challenging to forget about the problems of your students, or your school, or your fellow teachers, or the families you serve, especially if they are heart-wrenching as many of them are. This process seems to run counter against the process of engaging in empathy. But empathy can be draining and can leave you paralyzed, hence the term *compassion fatigue*. For reference, let's first define *emotional detachment*. The following definition is from Very WellMind.com (Cherry, 2021):

Emotional detachment refers to being disconnected or disengaged from the feelings of other people. This can involve an inability or an unwillingness to get involved in the emotional lives of other people.

This description seems to paint detachment as a "bad" process—after all, disconnection and disengagement could appear as synonymous to being callous. (They sound negative!) However, you, the caring educator, will need to practice detachment in order to maintain your emotional well-being and carry out your job functions effectively. Carrying the emotional baggage of other individuals' problems throughout your evening and night will cause restlessness, anxiety, and insomnia. In order to effectively help those you serve, you need to be able to detach—and detach as completely as possible.

At the most basic level, detachment involves "letting go." Worrying about other people's problems will not solve those problems. This does not mean avoiding allowing yourself to feel the pain of others and looking for solutions, but it is about setting boundaries and space for your own mental well-being. Note that emotional detachment is not about turning yourself into an unfeeling brute. Healthy emotional detachment is temporary avoidance—freeing yourself from guilt, shame, and bad feelings. The inability to temporarily let go can lead to immense exhaustion. It is important to allow yourself to empathize but not be overly consumed by everyone else's problems twenty-four hours a day, seven days a week! You can consider emotional detachment as another way of saying, "*I love me!*" Here are some strategies to facilitate emotional detachment at the end of each workday:

- Create a Worry Time: Set aside a "worry time" every day and do all your worrying during that time. Worry about everyone—empathize as much as you want! Ruminate as much as you would like to ruminate. But limit that worry time to no more than five minutes at the end of the day. Then detach, let go, and focus on the present. Someone brilliant once said: "Worrying about the future robs the present of happiness." There can be no space for joy if temporary emotional detachment is not engaged.
- Recognize when you cannot do anything to resolve the situation. Knowledge is indeed power—learn what you can control and what you cannot. Allow yourself five minutes to feel upset, and then move on. Imagine two big circles that overlap in the middle (a Venn

diagram). One circle consists of the area labeled "things you can control," and the other area is labeled "things that matter most"—the space where these two intersect is where your focus should be placed.
- Write it down and be done with it. Process your emotions (feeling angry or upset) by writing them down. Then toss the piece of paper down the garbage bin or watch it burn in your fireplace (carefully!). You have empathized; now it is time to think of your own well-being.

Emotional detachment is a healthy habit to develop. It can be helpful when you allow yourself to step out of the emotional situation and look at the event from a third-party, objective lens. Sometimes that is when solutions can be obtained, as we are sometimes handcuffed by our emotions and can't see the solutions as easily. Detachment is not avoidance. You cannot really control the situation in which a person finds himself or herself, nor what he or she does. Here is the danger of a failure to exercise emotional detachment regularly: You run the danger of losing the ability to experience joy. Additionally, you will become so emotionally exhausted that you reach the point of burnout. Here is a theory about why a significant percentage of teachers leave the profession before their first five years are over: It is because of a failure to achieve emotional detachment. This is a skill that needs to be practiced and developed; educators tend to carry the emotional pain of their students, and when you have anywhere from thirty to 160 students, that can be *a lot* to handle!

BACK TO HOPE AND REALISTIC OPTIMISM

Hope can spring forth when we are relaxed and free from paralyzing stress. And with hope, we can be realistically optimistic. The argument that some education experts have hoisted against hope is that it is not enough or it is deficient. Somehow this implies that hope is unnecessary, or that having hope leads to inaction. This is a dangerous notion, because hopelessness will lead to a lack of effort. Hardy (2020) stated that "hoping for something doesn't mean you're not taking action. Hope *is* action." This statement should be printed and framed in every school district superintendent's office. A true educational leader must first inspire hope among his or her staff if solutions to educational problems are to be found and/or implemented.

So, how does one inspire hope as a teacher or an educational leader? Model hope (*"I am hopeful that we will have good weather tomorrow so we can perform our lab...but if not, I have a plan for an indoor version. We will have fun either way!"*). Recount stories of hope thriving in the most deplorable situations. Use humor. Celebrate small wins in class, however silly they may be (*"Last weekend, I managed to do my laundry!"*)! Question negative predictions by engaging in realistic processing (*"What would be the chances of that bad event happening?"*). Be a trustworthy adult, because hope comes more easily when there is trust.

REFLECTION QUESTIONS

1. Why is realistic optimism different from unrealistic optimism?
2. How is hope a requirement for action? Why does hope = action?
3. Why do you need to decompress? How can you do it successfully?
4. Why is it necessary to emotionally detach, albeit temporarily?
5. What three things can you do tomorrow that will foster hope within you and among the people around you, including your students?

Chapter Six

Humor as a Pathway to Hope

Humor is powerful, and the utilization and appreciation of humor is undoubtedly essential in the navigation of one's social environment. We all remember those teachers who inspired us with jokes and stories that made us laugh. Those were the teachers who made us want to go to school and learn. Most educators (and administrators do know this) will find that students often gravitate to those instructors who always have a ready smile and who do not take themselves too seriously.

Teachers will also purposely walk two buildings away every day to spend precious lunch minutes with other staff members who possess sunny outlooks in life and have funny stories to share, because somehow these individuals make the remaining periods of the day doable (in spite of the exhaustion). In class, humor is many teachers' choice "weapon" of engagement, and for some, it is their most-effective classroom-management strategy. For most educators, humor also functions as a healthy coping strategy to handle the enormous stresses associated with teaching.

HUMOR, HOPE, AND REALISTIC OPTIMISM

There is evidence that humor is associated with increased feelings of hope. Vilaythong et al. (2003), in a study involving subjects between the ages of eighteen and seventy-six, found that watching funny videos increased hopeful feelings/states among the participants. It can be argued that if teachers are to increase students' optimism about their self-efficacy (including their ability to weather adversity), humor can be a strategy. Humor can relieve stress and promote an improved sense of well-being.

Hence, teachers who can see humor in adverse situations may face lower risks of burnout. In the figure below, humor is seen as a pathway to practicing realistic optimism, with hope as a moderator. Certainly, humor is one, among many, contributing variables to hope. A whole host of other positive constructs (e.g., resilience, gratitude) is postulated to result in higher levels of hope, and hence, optimism.

In this discussion, we distinguish humor from sarcasm. We know there is discomfort associated with the latter and pure joy with the former. Jokes made for the sake of just passing jokes can lead to harmful consequences, and under no circumstances should a teacher "pass jokes" that have the potential to offend or promote intergroup dissonance (Hodson & MacInnis, 2016). Some jokes have the potential to discriminate, ridicule, and promote group subservience. A teacher must always exercise caution in telling jokes by reflecting first on any unintended consequences from the sharing.

There are abundant articles that discount the usefulness and effectiveness of using humor in teaching. Hattie (2017), a well-renowned education researcher from Australia, conducted a meta-analytic review of robust studies on factors that influence student achievement. Humor was low on the list of his 256 influences, manifesting a very small effect size of 0.04 that reflects a likely positive effect on student achievement. Yet, common sense tells us that positive emotions resulting from the use of appropriate humor will make teaching and learning enjoyable. Humor promotes an emotional climate more conducive to learning as well as a safe environment. Students appear to be more highly motivated to engage in classwork that may otherwise be nonpalatable when humor is used. Humor does not only serve the purpose of making students laugh, but it also functions in building class cohesion.

Educator personal observations reveal that students interact more positively with each other when humor is utilized. Perhaps this is due to shared feelings of belonging to a joyful community. Perhaps you have had multiple occasions to hear students talk about teacher preferences or look at sample student evaluations of yourself and your peers. It is common to note how students indicate that a teacher's sense of humor is so often associated with student preference for the class. It may be argued that students find classwork "fun," not because the activity itself is fun. As the cognitive scientist Daniel Willingham (2009) stated, thinking is not really enjoyable, but if the teacher used humor in reframing the activity, it becomes fun and engaging for the student.

Although research on the effects of humor on student learning is inconclusive, an article from the American Psychological Association (2018) indicated many benefits to using humor (not the sarcastic variety) in a college classroom. Some of the indicated benefits included: (1) increased interest in learning tasks, (2) a reduction in anxiety and stress over the learning materials, (3) increased motivation in class, (4) openness to creative and divergent thinking, and (5) tightened psychological bonds among teachers and students. Perhaps a cheap and easy "weapon for mass instruction" is humor. It is not only good for students, but it likely also mitigates teacher stress and brings joy to the act of teaching.

A colleague teaching junior high students in a Title I (high-poverty) school recounts using humor in as many ways as she could because it was her survival mechanism and coping strategy. Humor allowed her to weather the stresses associated with teaching adolescents the whole day and feeling isolated from adults. She printed many quotes about humor and regularly posted them all over her workspace and walls to remind her that even if it was *just period 1*, she would last the subsequent four more periods if she kept a cheerful disposition. (She admits to being prone to also drinking copious amounts of coffee, at least one cup per period, before she discovered the power of humor.) Here are some of the posted statements and quotations she accumulated throughout her career:

- *"A day without laughter is a day wasted."*—Charlie Chaplin
- *"Humor is mankind's greatest blessing."*—Mark Twain
- *"Every time you are able to find humor in a difficult situation, you win!"*—Anonymous
- *"Humor can alter many situations and help us cope at the very instance we are laughing."*—Allen Klein
- *"A smile is like an instant face-lift!"*—Christie Brinkley
- *"Beauty is instantly more than doubled—ugliness, more than halved—by the mere act of smiling."*—Mokokoma Mokhonoana

The last two statements are definitely popular favorites! This teacher's commitment to humor is probably the reason she has not aged much in her looks! She attests that because of her commitment to smile, despite all the challenges the school year might bring, she has been coming home less emotionally exhausted. She shares that it is her strategy to start every class with smiles and laughter. She believes that spending five to seven minutes at the start of each class to set a positive emotional climate pays dividends. The whole period appears to move so much more smoothly and faster.

Here are some ways in which humor can be used to positively "manipulate" classroom climate and the emotional states of students for joyful learning:

1. *Storytelling-A-Lie:* This is a strategy in which the teacher shares a funny story; it may not be exactly 100 percent true, but it is embellished, dramatized, and exaggerated to elicit laughter from students. Self-deprecating humor seems to appeal to most students (particularly teenagers), and it is ideal for educators who love hearing themselves and others laugh at themselves. It starts with "inventing" stories about yourself (perhaps grounded in a little bit of truth), in which you fall flat on your face, or you deal with an awkward situation in which you gave the "wrong" answer or made a wrong assumption with hilarious consequences, etc.

   An educator's "storytelling-a-lie" strategy can also foster hope—as the ending always involves learning: *"Well, now I know I should not do that!"* Students see the storytelling teacher as a human being who makes mistakes, laughs it off, and moves forward. Students may start groaning (but at the same time smiling) whenever a teacher launches Mondays with: "Class, you won't believe what happened to me last weekend!" And yet, when that teacher pauses and says, *". . . Okay, never mind!"* all the students will beg that teacher to tell the story. Try it! It never fails! To make your stories truly funny, you should relish stating your narrative, engage in dramatic pauses—in short, pretend you are out to win an Oscar for your performance. Relish the moment, as everybody loves a story. Additionally, we all know that teaching itself is a performance art!

2. *Sassy One-Liners:* These could take the form of comebacks or unexpected quips. One time, while teaching the very interesting topic

of how to balance chemical equations (I'm using sarcasm here), a teacher noticed that her students' faces were exhibiting confusion and frustration. She looked at her board and was horrified to see that she had, for twenty minutes, taught the whole topic wrong! Horror of horrors, she realized then that she had just wasted precious instructional minutes . . . so she stopped, and with a very solemn and serious affect, admitted to her students (with a dramatic air of dejection) that she had taught the whole thing *erroneously!* Then, as she finished erasing the board (she had a large, long whiteboard), she stopped, faced the class, then said, with a straight face: "*Well, aren't you glad I am NOT a plastic surgeon? Because . . . that could have been your nose I just erased!*" The whole class laughed, and she began teaching the lesson once again—more intelligently and with 100 percent concentration this time!

Another favorite sassy one-liner that can be used frequently is the following: During high-stakes testing (district benchmarks, unit tests, etc.), when the class energy is tense and students are anxious, a teacher can deliberately say (ten minutes after the test has started): "Okay—time's up! Pass your papers in now." As you hear the gasps of disbelief, then casually say: "*Just kidding! I want you guys to stop, and if you can, close your eyes and take three deep breaths. Now that I have made you laugh, you can go on and continue taking the test—and believe that you have the knowledge and skills to excel.*" This combines humor, laughter, positive emotions—and hope for a possible best outcome. (Of course, you should not do this during state-mandated, high-stakes assessments!) Look for inspiration for sassy one-liners (appropriate ones, of course!) from videos of stand-up comedians. There are many on YouTube. Keep a notebook listing the ones you can use in the classroom.

3. *Appropriate Jokes in the Least Likely of Places.* Some teachers are fond of inserting short jokes, or stories that will elicit a smile, in highly unlikely places: on homework pages, at the end of tests, in reading articles, etc. As an example, a twenty-point quiz might end with a knock-knock joke. (This might elicit a groan, but it will always be followed by a smile.) The joke could be followed by an reminder to the students to check their work. This is quite powerful, as students, once in a positive frame of mind, are more motivated to indeed review their work.

One colleague sends homework that frequently has a joke inserted in the middle. He recounts having had some students on more than one occasion tell him that they actually look forward to the assignment because of the jokes. Whenever this teacher had to assign reading that's dry and apt to be described as "boring" (*but still must be read*)—typically these are nonfiction assignments—he would insert a joke in the middle, making it look just like the text!

It was the highlight of his day to hear the students groan, or laugh, snicker, or giggle, at different times during the reading, when they find that the teacher has again done the "funnies." You might ask, Is it disruptive? Not significantly...and if the task is boring, their minds will wander anyway. Educators will find that once students have had their laugh, they are actually more motivated to go back and finish the "boring" material. They will want to see if another joke has been surreptitiously inserted within the material.

4. *Presentations That Are Spiced Up with Humor.* Every educator loves using PowerPoint (or Google Slides) presentations for explicit direct instruction. However, these presentations can be very dry, monotonous . . . and *boring.* (Middle-school students usually have no qualms in letting teachers know this by yawning loudly during the presentation.) Another colleague of mine found a way to spice these presentations up by using celebrities' images with callouts (somewhat like memes but talking about the content). This colleague also knows how to use animations, or gifs. It is typical for her slides to have Beyonce sliding from left to right in the slide frame, teaching atomic theory. The next slide might have Tom Cruise hopping around to teach about electronegativity. To foster inclusion, she might include a football player, a *telenovela* actress, a rap singer, or a pop star (all appropriately attired, of course) doling out nuggets of chemistry wisdom. Is it somewhat distracting? Yes. Do the students still pay attention to the content? Yes. Do the students remember "electronegativity" better because Tom Cruise hopped around to explain it? Definitely! In fact, when one student claimed that this colleague did not accurately teach the lesson on electrons, he was promptly corrected by another student, who, with a straight face, said that she knew that she did—because Britney Spears had been dancing across the slide. (Yes, that surely dates all of us!)

There are many free, animated, celebrity gifs and clipart images available with a simple internet search. Exercise caution in downloading these images for classroom use, however, as some may be inappropriate or offensive.
5. *Games and Puzzles with a Humorous Solution.* Many eachers also love using games and puzzles in the classroom, as they spark joy. However, one teacher I know often re-creates them so there is a punchline to a joke as the solution. For example, he may use acrostics to review vocabulary knowledge of students. After solving about ten to twelve Tier III terms, he may number the letters in the students' solutions and ask them to decipher the last message at the bottom of the page by using these numbered letters.

This message will often ask them to do something (e.g., SMILE AT THE TEACHER . . . or AIR-FIVE THE TEACHER). This has the following added positive outcome: He knows when students have finished the puzzle, and he is also able to tease out a smile or a laugh. It is quite astonishing to see students who will not share answers because it has become a friendly competition in class to decipher what the teacher wants them to do at the end of the assignment!

Certainly there are many ways of bringing humor in the classroom. A fellow science teacher, Mr. TA, began calling his warmup tasks "*Warmup Fo-Shizzles.*" Many have borrowed this strategy and also started reframing potentially boring worksheets and quizzes. The teachers were astounded by how students reacted (positively)! These were the same problem sets teachers typically gave, but somehow the *Fo-Shizzle* moniker made it more engaging (and yes, there were giggles and groans). When there were no Warmup or Quiz Fo Shizzles, students even asked for them! Remember that humor can be content-integrated or not. Humor can also be intentional or spontaneous.

THE BEST STRATEGY: AVOID THE NEGATIVITY SUPERHEROES

One piece of advice that beginning teachers usually get (often whispered to them) is to avoid the faculty lounge at all cost. A visit to this "negativity" black hole in the school, as someone once called it, will always leave staff members feeling dejected. It is surprising that it takes teachers some time to realize that it is because a few educators (not all staff members—but a handful) whom you meet in the staff lounge while you are eating lunch or taking a break have the capacity to rob you of your joy and humor. After thirty minutes of lunch, teaching the rest of the periods became a tremendous struggle, all because one is forced to spend time with the one or two following characters:

- *Miserable Mindy*: This person views every situation as miserable and unbearable. Every conversation is peppered with a deep, mournful sigh and utterances of *"I can't wait to retire!"*
- *Grumpy Gary*: The face of this person says it all—even his "smile" is a smirk, and his attempts at humor are usually barbed with sarcasm.
- *Complaining Cathy*: There is no dearth of subjects and events about which this person cannot complain: the microwave, the copy machine, the custodian, the milk at the cafeteria . . . name it, and Cathy will complain about it!
- *Pessimistic Paul*: Every future situation is "gloom and doom" for Paul. He (or she) can drain any hope (and hence, joy) from anyone. Even good news is spun as a catastrophe waiting to happen.
- *"Against Administration and All" Anthony*: This person is like "Complaining Cathy," but more focused. Every single act or event is due to incompetent, ignorant, and ineffective administrators, from all levels of hierarchy. Some of his posits may be true, as incompetent administrators do exist; however, no accountability and no initiative is ever assumed to be positive by this person.
- *Blameful Betty*: Blameful Betty is the staff member who takes any bad situatio—and they are abundant—and blames everybody else for them. Watch out! This person is also fond of stabbing other staff members in the back, in her hunt to find someone to blame other than herself. Blameful Betty will lower her voice every time someone walks in, but she might still be heard—which mournfully, is often the case.
- *Antipathic Archie*: Antipathy may not be the worst of all sins, but it can also drain a person's energy. With "Antipathic Archie," the decision is always inaction, and the mood should always be one of resignation. No decisive action can ever be taken to solve any problem. And everything seems to be a problem!

Humor as a Pathway to Hope 83

- *Argumentative Annie*: Annie is easy to spot—she is the staff member who begins every statement with the word "*But . . .*" This staff member can turn every lunch period into a debate, as every statement can be twisted and reframed as a challenge to be argued against. She usually has a very loud voice, and she can talk over anyone. Any teacher who has the misfortune to connect with Annie will leave the faculty lounge emotionally exhausted and mentally drained.

From the above list, whom do you dread interacting with the most? Why? Create some responses for the people mentioned above.

Look at the figure below. Can you identify who among the "Negativity Superheroes" could be responsible for each comment? How would you respond? Are there any similarly negative comments you have heard in your own experience?

The characters listed above can be referred to as "Negativity Superheroes." They wear invisible capes to trap anyone who gets near enough, then suck them into the black hole of gloom and doom. Note that the term *superheroes* is used here to denote these persons' absolute power to transform the emotional climate of a group. Now, the whole faculty should *not* be a total blackhole of negativity, for there are those who are delightfully joyful, such as Positive Polly, Smiling Sam, Humorous Holly, and Optimistic Otis.

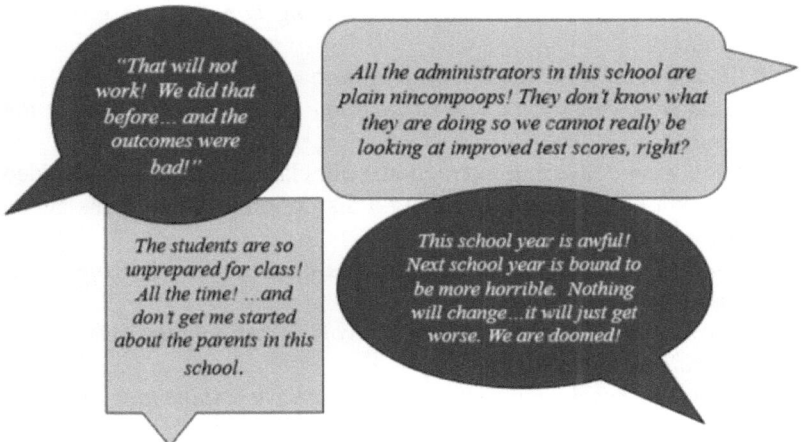

Figure 6.1. What You May Hear at the Faculty Lounge. Author created.

However, educators often attest that it seems these latter personalities are far outnumbered by the Negativity Superheroes, because the latter are louder and seem to possess more forceful personalities. It is typical in schools for the Optimism Bunch to stick together and meet up for lunch in someone else's classroom (usually the one with the microwave of the highest wattage) rather than to visit the Black Hole. Many educators have certainly done so for years, for their own mental well-being. It is definitely difficult to practice and teach realistic optimism if a person is surrounded by these Negative Superheroes hanging about!

CHECKING YOUR HUMOR QUOTIENT

Here is a situational humor questionnaire for teachers, based on the Situational Humor Response Questionnaire (SHRQ) developed by Martin and Lefcourt (1984). Note that this questionnaire appears to have been created by the authors as a self-reflection tool, not as a diagnostic instrument. The following questions have been created to mimic the situations depicted in the SHRQ to align with scenarios that might be encountered by an educator:

1. A lesson did not go as planned; in fact, it unfolded horribly. How do you react?
   a. *Get home as fast as you can, avoiding contact with everyone, and cry.*
   b. *Brush it off and blame it on bad luck.*
   c. *Laugh at yourself as you recall some funny episodes during the lesson.*
2. As you were delivering instruction, your class student clown decided to crack a harmless joke, causing a disruption as all students began laughing. What do you do?
   a. *Nothing! Just savor the moment and join in on the laughter, then move on.*
   b. *Frown, and in your most serious voice, castigate the class clown for disrupting the class.*
   c. *Send the mischievous student out and have a short talk with him/her.*

3. While being observed for an evaluation by your principal, all forms of technology vital to your effective delivery of the lesson went on dysfunction mode. What do you do?
    a. *Quietly curse your luck and hand your students their worksheets.*
    b. *Tell your students, while laughing: "Well, that just proves that technology can smell my fear!" (They should all have been aware that you were being observed . . .)*
    c. *Spend the next twenty minutes fumbling with switches and plugs in the hopes of getting the technology to work.*
4. You are driving home after a particularly exhausting meeting. During your drive time, what do you do?
    a. *Think about all the bad things that happened during the day.*
    b. *Clear your head and think about dinner.*
    c. *Make a conscious effort to focus on the positive events that happened during the day.*
5. Miserable Mindy, Complaining Cathy, and Antipathetic Archie dominated a school meeting that left you exhausted and deflated. As you reflect on the meeting, which reaction or response do you tend to adopt?
    a. *These are three staff members who are very negatively biased. While their opinions could be valued, they should not take any emotional space in my mind.*
    b. *I will dissociate and not reflect on what happened.*
    c. *Everything is bad. These staff members know what they are talking about. This school is doomed.*

You must have experienced each of these scenarios at some point, or a variation of them. While you cannot change the situation, your response should not lead to abject sadness and disillusionment, nor denial and dissociation from what happened. Your answers, hopefully, were the following: (1) c; (2) a; (3) b; (4) c; and (5) a.

Do you have any situation with which you are currently dealing that has left you feeling dejected? How can you use humor to be more optimistic about the situation? How can you use humor to uplift and inspire your students and colleagues?

FINAL WORDS

Teaching is difficult and exhausting enough: Use humor to mitigate distress and promote realistic optimism among your students and colleagues. Humor should have a place in your teaching toolbelt, for it is indispensable as a self-care tool!

Chapter Seven

Check Your Attitude to Boost Job Satisfaction

Have you ever been told to "check your attitude," or alternatively, have you ever told someone *they* needed to check *their* attitude? Have you ever thought that some of your friends, family members, or colleagues could do themselves some good if they just took the time to review and then adjust their attitudes? But what is attitude? In psychology, attitude has a special meaning. Verywellmind.com defines *attitude* as "a set of beliefs, feelings, and behaviors toward a specific person, object, event, or thing. Opinions and beliefs shape attitudes" (https://www.verywellmind.com/attitudes-how-they-form-change-shape-behavior-2795897; Cherry 2021).

Someone has probably asked you to identify your attitude toward certain rules and policies at your school, district, or workplace. For example, you may have been asked: What is your attitude toward requiring students to wear school uniforms? What is your attitude about adjunct duties? What is your attitude about some teachers releasing their students a few minutes early for lunch? What is your attitude about parents complaining straight to the principal without communicating with the teacher first? It turns out that our attitude influences our patterns of behavior significantly, and consequently, it influences how satisfied we are about our jobs and ultimately our happiness (more about job satisfaction later)!

Using the figure below, consider how many teachers use attitude in a myriad of ways and how nuances in meaning exist. How does each of these statements display a different utilization of perceptions about attitude?

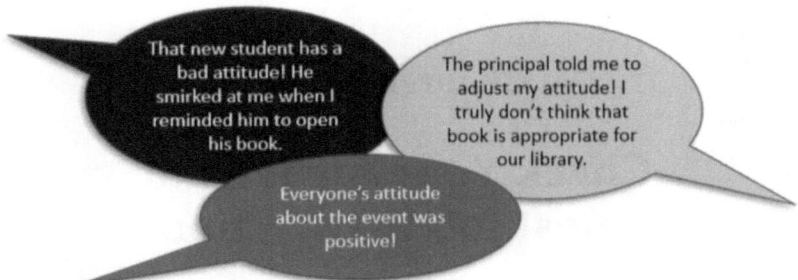

Figure 7.1. We Use Attitudes in Different Ways. Author created.

WHAT MAKES UP AN INDIVIDUAL'S ATTITUDE?

Attitudes can be explicit or implicit. As the description implies, explicit attitudes are not hidden and are displayed via language and behavior. The individual is also very much aware of his or her attitude. The opposite is true for implicit attitudes, which are underneath the surface and the person is unconscious of them. Nevertheless, these attitudes still exert an influence on one's thinking and behavior. Attitude has three components, but when we speak of attitude, we often speak only about one of these components. Here are the three components of attitude, represented by the letters A, B, and C:

1. **Affective component**: This component refers to how one feels about the subject. It almost always goes unnoticed, but it is a significant influencer of behavior.
2. **Behavioral component**: This refers to the actions in which you engage because of your attitude. For example, if one has a bad attitude toward school, disrespectful behavior toward teachers may result. If a student has a good attitude about math, that student is consequently going to be more participative in (and apt to derive more joy from) math classes.
3. **Cognitive component**: This refers to one's thinking, that is, an individual's thoughts and beliefs about the person, thing, object, or event.

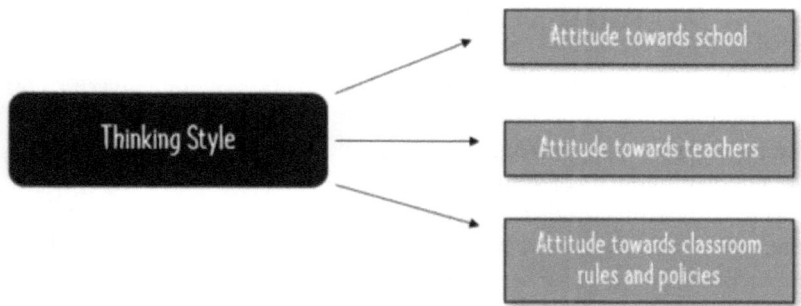

Figure 7.2. Thinking Styles and Attitudes. Author created.

Attitude seems to be very similar to our thinking styles (see figure 7.2 above). Yes, it is definitely associated with our thinking styles, but while thinking styles are more permanent, attitudes can be quite short in their lifespan. Thinking styles also encompass our emotions. A person's thinking style can drive or frame that individual's attitude toward a specific object, event, or person. It is possible that within one's thinking style, different sets of attitudes can result. Attitude is learned and can be explicit or implicit, as explained above. The "in your face" attitudes are explicit; examples include a student throwing a pencil or refusing (with much fanfare) to do any classwork. Some attitudes are harder to discern; those are implicit attitudes.

Attitudes develop from experiences, social factors (which could be cultural), learning, observation, and conditioning. Because one's environment is very much a component of one's experiences, the people around you help shape your attitude. Tap back into your past and present and think about how this has shaped your attitude. Think about your attitudes toward teaching and learning and ask why you possess these attitudes:

- *Do you value education?*
- *Why did you go into teaching (or your current profession)?*
- *Do you feel that teachers should be lifelong learners?*

FROM ATTITUDES TO BEHAVIOR

There is an assumption that attitudes significantly shape behavior and that people engage in actions that align with their attitudes about certain subjects, events, or persons. This may be true in most instances, but social psychologists have revealed that behaviors do not always necessarily align with attitudes. It seems that the context or situation in which the actions are engaged drives alignment or misalignment. Think about a student who "*gives you the hand*" and declares s/he does not really care about school. This action may not necessarily reflect the student's overall attitude (not caring about school). Instead, it may be a coping strategy to protect oneself from failure. Or the behavior may reflect an attempt to align with certain peers and gain their approval.

The strength with which an attitude is held is aligned with the consistency of how that attitude will influence behavior. The strength of an attitude depends on the following:

1. *Importance of the subject to the person.* How relevant or meaningful is the subject? How important is the individual to the person? My attitude toward school and teaching in general is strong because I believe in its importance toward attaining equity.
2. *Knowledge about the subject, event, or person.* The more knowledgeable an individual is about the subject or event or person, the stronger the attitude will be. An expert on reading instruction will have a stronger attitude toward a certain reading program and will likely engage in behaviors that manifest his or her preference.
3. *Personal experience.* Attitude is also influenced by an individual's personal experience with the situation, subject, or person. Think about how we all have different attitudes about math. Some love it; some loathe it! Our own personal experiences must have shaped these attitudes.

In some cases, people will change their attitudes to fit their actions, as there is discomfort when attitudes and behaviors are not aligned. *Cognitive dissonance* is the term used to describe this discomfort or unpleasant feeling. Those attitudes that people possess with greater confidence

> **Attitude about former students:** Do you listen to former teachers who share their attitudes about students/classrooms? Does this influence your own attitude about these student/s or classrooms?
> **Attitude about administrators:** Do you or other colleagues express your/their attitude about administrators? How does this influence how you feel and think about the administrators?
> **Attitude about parents:** Similarly, do you get "warnings" about certain parents? How do these attitudes influence how you interact with these parents?

Figure 7.3. Self-Reflection Questions about Your Attitudes. Author created.

tend to "stick more" and are more highly predictive of behavior, compared to attitudes that are questionable to the individual and not held with great tenacity. Cognitive dissonance is the phenomenon in which actions do not match the attitude, and it is distressing. To relieve the discomfort, individuals may change their attitude or the behavior/s. Study the table below, displaying cognitive dissonance examples in education:

Table 7.1.

Attitude	Behavior/s
Student declares a hatred for math.	Stays after school with the teacher to get extra help.
Teacher believes ADHD is a "made-up" disorder.	Engages strategies in the classroom that include incorporating more movement and lessen distractions.
Administrator does not believe that gifted children need a "separate" program to address their needs.	Organizes a committee of teachers to discuss what program might be implemented to support differentiated instructional options for GATE (gifted and talented) students.

Can you think of other examples? Look at each case above, and predict how the individual might resolve his/her cognitive dissonance exemplified in each case.

A BAD ATTITUDE CAN BE EXHAUSTING!
HACKING ATTITUDE FOR HAPPINESS

Do you have the "seventh sense" of being able to recognize when you are developing a bad attitude and immediately call yourself to task? Many people don't possess this inner voice. Most of us don't have this inner critic (we possess the other kinds!), and that may mean it is quite easy to adopt a negative attitude about anything. Instead of being fleeting, a bad attitude can end up ruining our day, draining joy out of the things we do, and contaminating other people's attitudes. There is also the possibility that your own bad attitude can rub off on other people (attitude contagion?).

Because people who possess a positive attitude generally enjoy life more and are often happier and more successful than those who go through the day with a negative attitude, it makes sense to learn to recognize when we are having (or about to develop) a bad attitude and then address it. Our attitudes can constitute a significant influential force in our lives—it can either motivate us and the people around us to do wonderful things or cause us (and the people around us) to "catch" the bad attitude and be as miserable as we are (and engage in problematic behavior). Here are some ways to address your bad attitude before it ruins your day, or week, or month:

1. *Look for role models.* There are certainly many individuals who possess good attitudes, although the ones with bad attitudes tend to stick out as they seem to be more vocal in their expressions of discontent. Because of our negativity bias, perhaps we are more sensitive to their presence. These are the teachers who, during staff meetings, whisper loudly (I know that is not quite possible, but they do!) about how cruel the world is, and how they hate this policy and that or this administrator or that. Before you know it, you are swept up in the frenzy and are feeling distraught and hating your job, as well.

   Look for the ones who are not like them. These are the teachers who do not need to whisper (loudly) because their body language exudes their attitude. Even with the delivery of bad news, these teachers are able to reframe the situation to be a blessing. These are the individuals in the faculty lounge who are more patient, smile more often, and are more optimistic. This is the attitude we want to "catch." If those with good, healthy attitudes are not present in our social circles, we must find them.

2. *Arrest that bad attitude and think about how it will affect your day!* Develop the self-awareness or capacity to realize when you are having an attack of the negative suds. Pay attention to how you receive news, for example, or how you respond to events beyond your control. Once you recognize that you are about to adopt a negative attitude, stop and think. Is the situation *really* all that bad? Also, if you do succumb to being grumpy or accusatory or hateful, where will that attitude take you? You'll be more tired at the end of the day, and you will miss out on the many little blessings that actually come your way.

Imagine having a radar that alerts you when a bad attitude is about to take over your psyche. You stop, and you think. *Oohhh . . . I do not really like that policy. I am so angry. I will tell her what a dunce she is for even thinking of this* (STOP HERE): *Hmmm, let me think about that policy change again. What could be the reason they made the change? Should I not try to find out first before I let myself go down the rabbit hole of despair?* If this "***Recognize → Stop → Think***" step does not occur, think of how your whole day, and perhaps the whole week, would go! You would probably be miserable, and this misery would be contagious. You would be angry all weekend and would end up with a list of people or other things to be mad about. This attitude can easily become all-consuming.

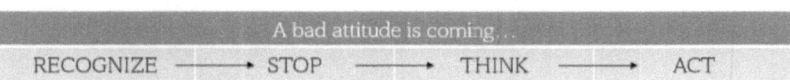

Figure 7.4. Holding a Space for an Attitude Check. Author created.

3. *Be proactive and not reactive!* Do not be a hostage to the emotions of others or to your own impulse to react with your emotions immediately. Do not give up your power to think and feel for yourself by becoming a puppet to the emotions and thoughts of others. When someone says something that is upsetting, take a moment to reflect on the message. First, did you hear it correctly? Second, is your interpretation accurate? Second, analyze the message and/or event—what is making you distressed or discombobulated? If

your supervisor has said something upsetting to you, stop and think. What exactly was said? Write it down and deconstruct the message. Is your interpretation correct? Are you clear about the message, or do you need more information? Do not always be a hostage to what someone else wants you to feel.

Do bad attitudes rule your workplace? Do you find that your students have picked up on these attitudes and are reflecting them back to peers and adults? Here are some signs and symptoms of this occurring:

- Constant gossip and complaining
- Disregarding new ideas from other colleagues
- Feeling exhausted most hours of the day
- Disrespecting other people (e.g., snapping at others)
- Not paying attention during discussions and meetings
- Intolerance for constructive critique

If you are a contributing factor, here are some additional ways to hack your bad attitude:

1. I am responsible for getting what I need and want.
2. Good things happen to those who expend the effort to make them happen.
3. I can be flexible and adapt quickly.
4. I know how to keep going when things get rough.
5. Complaining will not solve things—I need to be part of the solution.

JOB SATISFACTION AND BURNOUT

There are areas outside your control that impacts job satisfaction. For example, compensation is one of those variables that can influence how you feel about your job, and it may be outside your control to negotiate the salary you feel aligns with your talents and skills. While getting a monthly salary that is fair or more than fair will certainly influence how much you love your job, it is surprisingly not the singular, most significant factor in guaranteeing joy and satisfaction in the workplace.

A fellow educator with thirty years of experience has recently risen to the ranks of the salary schedule (with a fancy title to go along with it), and she felt the thrill at every step. In 2008, she bypassed the six-figure mark! For a migrant educator who started teaching in the United States, this was such an accomplishment!

However, the feeling of happiness was not lasting. She was working 225 days, and being on salary, she was also expected to deliver work at all times—even on the weekends—at the drop of a hat. She was often delivering workshops until 6:00 p.m., cleaning up after these workshops and designing and creating them during the weekends. The reports, associated with accountability for funding received, brought her no joy— this work sucked the joy out of her days and took very long to develop, with many edits required.

In all honesty, she intimated that she would rather grade 150 science lab reports than write the state or federal reports, which she knew would be returned three times after their submission to be tweaked so it would pass whoever is reviewing it at the federal level. While being with kids and students guaranteed laughter for her, having her days consumed by endless meetings for a six-figure salary did not give her the happiness she sought. In fact, she found her happiness when she was called to sub (on an emergency), as it gave her a chance to reconnect to her teaching roots.

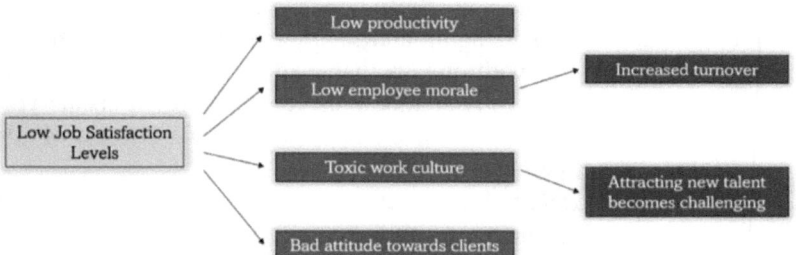

Figure 7.5. Job Satisfaction: Symptoms and Outcomes. Author created.

So, what truly brings joy and predisposes one to have an optimistic mindset? Here is a list. Check off those items that are not surprising to you. Find the one that most resonates with you.

1. *Social Connections*: Those who are highly introverted may find this surprising, but for most people, teaching buddies (and staff and administrators, too) are essential to job satisfaction. These are the ones you frequently sit beside during faculty meetings (including those meetings that could have been an email). Yes, that person or two who would join you as you engage in immature message conveyance (passing secret notes) about something only the two or three of you would find funny. The ones who bring happiness are oftentimes those educators with whom you would snatch fifteen minutes of your lunch period to vent and commiserate with about your problems.

   These coconspirators (colleagues) would be happy to listen to you talk endlessly about any person who happened to have given you a bad taste in the mouth or left you feeling annoyed. This circle of friends might include the one across the hall who would willingly check on your class if you are absent and need to use a sub (and for whom you would do the same). She or he is also the one who would give up a great class schedule so you could have a manageable load. Perhaps, she or he would also willingly watch over the last five minutes of your class so you could skedaddle to the parking lot and escape the traffic jam of dismissal for another appointment.

   Yes, social connections matter a lot in the education world. Countless studies have revealed how these friendships mitigate the levels of teaching stress. These are those bonds you make because you go through the same challenging and happy experiences together and can truly empathize with one another. Sadly, a six-figure salary in administration does not guarantee these connections. It seems you lose this circle once you enter the supposedly "dark" world of administration (but perhaps not).

2. *Purpose and Meaning*: Remember that feeling you get when you see students' faces light up because a lesson clicked or made sense? That look that fleets across students' faces signifies that their brains are hard at work trying to make meaning out of your fantastic lesson? Yes, that look. That smile. And sometimes, the unbridled blurting out of "Ahhhh . . . I get it!" There is nothing more satisfying than the positive feeling of joy that comes from knowing your work matters.

   Teachers live for these moments, and for those occasions when students, all grown up, return to your classroom to thank you. The

handmade cards with flowers plucked from the field next to the school, given by students who do not possess the means or resources to buy gifts, are the ones you save in a box to reopen and reread when things get rough. These are the signs that frequently remind you of your purpose and the meaning of the work you do! Keep these mementoes as they bring pure joy!
3. *Altruistic Involvement*: How can teachers still be expected to offer more? It turns out that doing good (e.g., volunteering) through participation in school events and activities is a factor that often contributes to job satisfaction. Many teachers attest to how exhausting it is to chaperone a dance or field trip or organize a street cleanup! However, these opportunities can tighten your connection to the school community, promote a positive school culture, and bring a strong sense of camaraderie. Several district office administrators have revealed that they miss these opportunities as they realize how much these "adjunct duties" actually bring joy! Well, there is always a need for more volunteers, so administrators, abandon the suits and volunteer as a crossing guard (carrying traffic stop signs do not go well with suits and ties) or in some other capacity.

This list is definitely not exhaustive. There are other variables that influence job satisfaction, such as workplace culture, support from administration, and having a kind, supportive supervisor who values you and has faith in you. But the factors listed above may trump everything else, and they are very actionable items. Regarding workplace culture, ask yourself whether the school climate is such that it breeds joy among staff that helps mitigate both emotional and physical exhaustion. If the answer is no, know that you have an influence over the workplace climate. Try answering the following self-reflection questions to evaluate your workplace culture, based on your perceptions (after all, your perceptions are your realities):

1. How do you feel about your workplace's (school's) culture?
2. Do you feel connected with other staff members at your school?
3. How open to change is your school and/or district?
4. Does your supervisor value your input?
5. Is communication from your school administrators timely and effective?

How much of the satisfaction from your job can come from you, what you actually do? The good news is you can hack joy, much like you can learn realistic optimism. Any day is a great day to start. If you find yourself exhausted to the point of being unable to find any joy in what you do, there are some steps you can take to rediscover that spark.

First, ask yourself: What is causing you to be emotionally exhausted? Name it and write it down. You can also use a protocol for finding the root causes, and consequently solutions. The 5-WHY protocol for determining root causes may be useful for this. It is a simple system that allows an individual to analyze a problem with improved clarity. At each stage, ask yourself: *How can you avoid, lessen, or mitigate these root causes?*

Here's an example:

PROBLEM: *I am so emotionally drained.*
STEP 1. Why? *I am left just doing reports. I am stuck at the office doing tasks that are absolutely unenjoyable.*
STEP 2. Why? *Because no one else would do it, so I am stuck with it.*
STEP 3. Why? *Well, because I volunteered to help my boss.*
STEP 4: Why? *Because my boss is dealing with so many issues related to the pandemic, and this is one way I can help. I feel bad for him.*
STEP 5: Why? *I care about the mental health of my boss and the people I work with. So, to spare them this joyless task, I took over.*

You can see that the 5-Why process is relatively easy, but it requires being honest with yourself. We can use these steps to reclaim our joy (which all of us lost during the pandemic) and thus mitigate our emotional exhaustion. At each step above where an answer to each *Why* is provided, a possible solution is indicated. These responses refer to the same example above:

1. **First WHY**—Solution: *Perhaps I can take little breaks to disrupt the monotony of the work. Plus, not all aspects of the report writing are horrible—there are parts that are enjoyable, such as researching evidence for practice, generating and displaying data, analyzing data. These are areas that are actually fun (yes, I do enjoy them), and these tasks allow me to improve my research and data analysis skills.* (Note here that the person is taking control; a shift in thinking has happened!)

2. **Second WHY**—Solution: *Is this really true? Are there pieces that others can help with?* Maybe there is a wonderful secretary who is highly skilled and can help edit the document and check on the formatting. We have a technology coordinator who also loves doing research and knows a lot about the parent population. She is also a whiz at data visualization. (Note that the person is now tapping on resources who can help!)
3. **Third WHY**—Solution: There is really no solution here as the person cannot "unvolunteer"—that would be cruel, not compassionate, and irresponsible. So, the individual could instead choose to savor the positive feelings and knowledge that she is helping the boss and the team. She can relish (during her decompression time) the many times her boss has expressed his gratitude, both privately and publicly! She can intentionally find joy at having the opportunity to be collaborative and lessen the load of someone else! (Note that the person is now engaging in *reframing*.)
4. **4th WH**—Solution: *Same as above; I can find joy in knowing I am helping someone in need!*
5. **5th WHY**—Solution: No need for a solution! The person just needs to remind herself that she is a good person—a collaborator who cares about others—and celebrate that every time she feels dejected.

Try the 5-WHYs and solution protocol here. Complete the table below.

Table 7.2. Self-Exercise

PROBLEM: I do not find joy in my work anymore (example).		
1st Why?	Answer:	Solution:
2nd Why?	Answer:	Solution:
3rd Why?	Answer:	Solution:
4th Why?	Answer:	Solution:
5th Why?	Answer:	Solution:

Read all you have written in the second column. They may be the root causes of the problem. The third column provides action steps you can take. Now try the protocol again, but this time, use a real problem that has been plaguing you. Commit to being solution-focused by following the action steps in your solutions column.

To successfully escape the negative feelings about your job, it is not enough to look for the root causes. The approaches you engage must span across three domains of potential action: cognitive (adjusting your way of thinking); affective (altering the way you choose to feel); and behavioral (physical actions that mitigate the dissatisfaction and increase the level of joy). This was manifested in the 5-Why example. Let's look at the same dilemma experienced by a district office colleague, shared in the previous example and repeated here.

> *I hate my job. I feel useless because all I do is write these joy-draining reports for the state and federal dollars we receive. All we have discussed the past two years is the pandemic, and nothing about teaching and learning, which is what brings me joy. Everyone around me (mostly teachers) are also exhausted and miserable. I want to quit.*

Addressing a part of her dilemma—how she dislikes writing the state-mandated and federal reports—requires looking at the three dimensions and engaging in some reframing, as mentioned in the last step of the "5 Why" example.

1. Cognitive: The cognitive reframing may sound like this: "*I need to get a grip on these negative thoughts. The reports are truly not a joy to write, but they are important. Not working on or submitting the reports could mean a loss of funding, and my district is counting on me to do this work and ensure we are compliant.*"
2. Affective: The affective reframing could manifest in this way: "*I just don't like writing all these reports. But perhaps I don't hate all aspects of the task. True, I hate the actual physical act of sitting down, reviewing the template, reading the instructions, and the actual task of writing. However, there are parts of it that bring me joy: looking at data, analyzing the student survey data, and reading student comments. (I can see how much they love their teachers! Additionally, a good number of them declared actual love for math! These comments bring me joy.) Arranging focus interviews with parents and*

teachers also brings me joy as they foster and strengthen relationships. I can choose to focus on those emotions!"
3. Behavioral: Behavioral reframing includes actions that the person can actually undertake, including chunking the tasks into multiple phases, so she is not overwhelmed with writing them. Or creating a manageable timeline so that things are not rushed. She can also look at all the reports and find similarity among the sections, so she does not end up duplicating her efforts. And as the example above showed, she can enumerate a list of persons whose strengths can be leveraged to help write the reports.

In the book *Switch by Heath and Heath* (2010), a huge favorite among educators, the authors advocated a technique called *"shaping the path."* This means altering the environment so the desired behaviors (feelings and thinking) are achieved. In the dilemma articulated above, perhaps changing certain things about the workspace could cause a change in the teacher's attitude toward writing so it is not as unpleasant of a task as perceived. Soft music, mood lighting, papers and colored pens nearby, and a closed door so she can concentrate might help! *Can you think of approaches that would help shape your environment so things you must do but don't bring joy to you at least do not distress you?*

THE BADGE OF EMOTIONAL EXHAUSTION

The education culture—perhaps even our whole society—seems to value exhaustion. There appears to be a sense of pride associated with wearing the badge of exhaustion. If you are like most educators, you probably feel guilty when you don't volunteer for as many committees as humanly possible. It is likely that as you are reading this book, you are already thinking about all the events and committees you could help facilitate during the next academic year. You have also probably often observed teachers and administrators saying: *"I'll do it!"* and *"I'll take care of it!"* Many times, these people already have too many tasks on their plates! What could motivate people in schools and offices to work themselves to the point of pure exhaustion? As you read this, you are probably realizing you are one of those who decided to take on too much and your plate is now overflowing. There may be several reasons for this:

- *Fear of missing out*: In today's society, where we are bombarded by social media posts flaunting so many individuals doing incredible things, this may be a significant driver of the behavior of taking on too many tasks. Understandably, an individual wants to be part of the "action." We believe that if we don't assume responsibility for some part of the process, we will miss out on the rewards associated with advanced perceived success. We feel we must at least participate, but what likely ends up happening is that we take on a significant share of the responsibilities. We also may fear being branded as not being a "team player," or not wanting to collaborate. And that would be added to the already-exhausting pile of grading, designing lessons, preparing for labs, delivering instruction, and all other adjunct duties assigned.
- *Guilt*: Guilt is a strong emotion and a definite driver of behavior. If we do not volunteer and someone else does, we may suffer from feelings of remorse. *Why didn't I help? What will my colleagues think? They will probably assume I am too lazy or unwilling to contribute.* As stated above, guilt about being perceived as not a team player can play into this behavior. Guilt is associated with so many other unpleasant emotions (shame, for example) that most of us would rather be dead-tired than bear the burden of guilt.
- *Pride*: There is a satisfying feeling knowing we are so competent that we can juggle many projects at the same time. We may be anticipating feeling accomplished and having colleagues astounded at how we can easily accomplish many tasks at once and be successful at all of them (*at least this is what we are predicting*). We will show everyone that we can successfully handle multiple tasks, even if it means we have to sacrifice several weekends and spend them at school. But think of the pride (and happiness) we will feel at the end of a job (or multiple jobs) well done. However, is this really worth burning ourselves out for? And are we really setting a good example for our friends and family? Pride can be a double-edged sword.
- *Gaslighting*: Are you being made a victim of gaslighting? Is the person making the request for you to take on one more responsibility actively making you feel that you are the only one who can do it, so you have no other recourse but to say yes? Do they tell you that only you are perfect for the job, and no one else has the knowledge and skills? That it will be a "*piece of cake*" for you? That it will be a

"feather in your cap"? Are you being gaslighted into thinking that it was actually your idea in the first place? As an overworked teacher, staff member, or administrator, you may find it worthwhile to examine the nature of the request and dissect the language of how the request is being made.

SELF-REFLECTION QUESTIONS

1. Do you find yourself volunteering (even if you really don't want to) for extra tasks and duties, despite a lack of time and energy?
2. Why? Is it because of a fear of losing out? Feelings of shame and guilt? Pride? Were you gaslighted?
3. What are some ways you can resist the temptation of accepting one more responsibility?

THE ART OF SAYING NO

It is recommended that teacher preparation programs include a course on how to say no to adjunct duties and avoid physical and emotional exhaustion. You may laugh at this suggestion, but not being able to say no contributes to stress and leads to physical and emotional burnout! Some ways to do this include:

- *Just say, "No, sorry I cannot do it." You do not need to explain.*
- *"I am sorry, but I can't." You don't have to explain why.*
- *"I'm sorry, my plate is very full right now."*
- *"Sadly, unless you want me to **not** help struggling students after school, I cannot do it."*
- *"If you want to pull me out of lunch and bus duty, I can do it."* (Think of other duties you have where your help is critical, and you cannot be spared.)
- *"Some other time perhaps? This is not a good time for me right now."*

Emotional exhaustion is not, and should never be, a badge of honor. There should be no joy or pride that comes with stress and absolute, bone-numbing tiredness. Teachers and other educators are susceptible to emotional exhaustion because they are in the caregiving profession. They feel that there is an expectation that they will continue giving and giving and that they can sustain such heavy workloads because it is the nature of the job. Teaching is also an isolating profession. Teachers and other staff members are with children most hours of the day so that social support from adult peers can be lacking due to limited opportunities to interact. And because teaching is so exhausting, all an individual typically wants to do is go home at the end of a tiring day (*and all days are tiring!*). And yet, husbands, wives, and partners of teachers (and probably those of nurses, too) will be the first to tell you that all educators can talk about after getting home are classroom-related subjects.

Lack of control can be a significant contributor to emotional exhaustion. Teaching used to be quite enjoyable because there was a lot of freedom (autonomy) to be creative. There are some countries where teachers are free to choose their own curriculum program (textbooks) and develop their own scope and sequence in teaching. Also, teachers are allowed to design their own summative assessments. Most teachers naturally prefer collaborating with other staff members on these tasks because of the amount of work involved. In other countries, there is zero possibility of being evaluated for teaching effectiveness using state (government-mandated) assessments.

In the United States, however, such freedoms may not exist (depending on the state). Most teachers do not have a lot of freedom in designing their instruction because they are constantly advised to stick to the curriculum (hence the phrase that most teachers are sick of: *fidelity to the curriculum*), even if the curriculum is not effective. Worse, in California, that district-curriculum "marriage" lasts seven to eight years! Teachers must teach from a district-mandated textbook program and follow a scope and sequence or pacing guide, and the strictness with which this is enforced seems to be correlated to how many low-income families are in the demographics of the district.

Most teachers are required to administer the district assessments that usually are purchased from a vendor, as well as administer the high-stakes test assessments in the spring. And even if a teacher's classes deliver good results, she or he will still (most likely) not be allowed the freedom to design learning experiences for students without these parameters. Note that not all districts operate this way, but those that do cause more unhappiness for their educators.

Another reason for emotional exhaustion is just the tremendous amount of work associated with being an educator. BetterUp (2022) identifies teachers as being at high risk for burnout, along with social workers, ER technicians, healthcare workers, and financial managers. The work of a teacher never stops: Grading papers, communicating to parents, following board directives, and tutoring struggling students are all part of the job, on top of the actual teaching that takes place five to six hours every day.

The 2020–2022 school years have been brutal to all educators, with a greater number of disrespectful students, disgruntled parents (usually over masking and vaccinations), and emotionally explosive board meetings! We have seen numerous pickets and protests over mask and vaccination mandates at schools where hapless teachers and administrators are targeted—and yet, we were not the ones responsible for such mandates! We have personally seen many teachers break down and burst into tears. No wonder so many teachers, administrators, and school staff are declaring burnout! Other countries do not require five or more hours of actual teaching daily from staff. It seems teachers in the United States are an exception.

RECLAIMING THE JOY

One day, an administrator was visiting a classroom to be a guest teacher for Mrs. Ferraro. He arrived early and prepared for the presentation, but she was having some technology problems accessing her email and downloading the presentation. Her students waited patiently, but both adults could tell the students were beginning to get antsy. Mrs. Ferraro faced her thirty fifth-grade students and said, "Go outside and run a couple of laps. Then come right back here." The administrator expected a myriad of groans and complaints, but what he heard were shrieks of delight! All of Mrs. Ferraro's students happily "escaped" the classroom and indeed ran two laps around the campus! This provided enough time for them to finish finagling with the technology! When all the students returned, they were panting and had rosy cheeks and smiling faces. They dutifully sat down and focused on the presentation. Many kudos to Mrs. Ferraro! *What a creative idea, and who would have thought?*

So, what is the lesson behind this story? Joy can be reclaimed quite simply! It does not happen through big, bold acts that we have to engage, nor through shallow and fake team-building activities. Nor should reclaiming joy cost a lot of money (although perhaps a staff cruise through the Mediterranean could help!)—but through simple acts. The other day, a colleague was in charge of presenting the opening session of a PD, and she was in a quandary. The teachers were tired, overwhelmed, and unhappy. It was February, and teacher morale was low. Furthermore, everyone was just tired of the pandemic and the constant, never-ending cycle of contact tracing and isolating.

The welcome session was supposed to be a discussion of the different tiers of intervention and redefining the services at each tier. The presenter included (with much thought and agony) two inspiring videos that she hoped would make teachers realize how much they were valued. (The district was also in the midst of a highly contentious negotiation period with the classified and certificated bargaining groups.) It was an impossible "damned if you do and damned if you don't" situation. Until . . . the team gave the administrator a brilliant idea! Why not just surprise all teachers with thirty minutes of a mental health break instead of the welcome session? So, she opened the Zoom meeting for the Welcome Session with one slide that contained one word: *Surprise!*

The superintendent told them there would be basically no Welcome Session, and instead, their homework was to take the thirty minutes to: (a) take a walk, (b) hug their pets, (c) gossip with a friend, (d) drink some hot cocoa and play Wordle, or (e) do anything that constituted a mental health break for them! The results were heartwarming: Teachers, staff members, and principals all sent cabinet pictures of them drinking coffee, taking a walk, doing some stretching exercises, playing with their dogs, etc. That simple act brought a lot of joy! And it did not cost any money at all. Everyone went to the second Zoom session refreshed, ready to learn, and on time, with smiles on their faces.

We own the responsibility for our own joy and happiness, and yet we also engage in actions that hijack those blessings of joy. If you wish to avoid burnout, you must thoughtfully plan for those actions that bring you joy! Go take a walk during recess—ask your principal or district administrator to sub for you for ten to twenty minutes and go outside and take a walk! Don't take yourself so seriously. Surround yourself with good, positive company. Solve puzzles! Invest in a coloring book with a good set of crayons and lie in bed coloring. Watch "feel good" movies! Decompress and detach! Think optimistically (with a dose of realism).

Here are some other ways to reclaim joy. Check a few that you can do and pencil them into your calendar. Don't wait for the summer break to recharge; make a daily habit of engaging in joyful activities:

- *Meditate.* Find two minutes alone and do nothing. Clear your head. Do this at each start of the day. Check out http://www.donothing for2minutes.com/, and take two minutes to still your mind while listening to the sound of crashing ocean waves.
- *Keep your life simple.* Declutter your home and your classroom. Do not feel pressured to have Pinterest-worthy classroom decorations. Do not aspire to be an expert in using ten or more teaching apps and programs. Do not think that you should have twenty pieces of technology or devices to make your teaching effective. The more "things" you accumulate, the more exhausted you become because you need to learn how to use all of them and teach your students how to use them, and consequently, the less happy you will feel.
- *Slow down!* Not everything on the pacing guide must be "covered." Slow down and savor those moments when you can literally feel your students learning as you walk around your classroom. Listen to the wonderful noise and chaos of the classroom!
- *Wake up thirty minutes early and take a walk.* Savor the sights and sounds of the early morning when everything is quiet. Visualize how wonderful the day will unfold. How can it be otherwise? Take time to build a positive attitude at the start of the day. Breathe and stretch!
- *Keep a journal.* Write down three things to celebrate at the end of each day. Dissect the day's events and find every bit of blessing you can. It could be the littlest thing—but write it down! During those times when you can barely force yourself to wake up and face the day, get that journal out, randomly pick any day, and read what blessings you experienced during that day!
- *Rekindle the passion you feel for your profession.* Acknowledge that by teaching, you are serving others. The work is hard and sometimes unrewarding, but you never know when your influence will have a significant impact on someone else's life. Look for stories that

reaffirm how important your life of service is! You truly are making a difference—you just can't tell how far your reach has been.
- *Choose to make someone else smile and be contagious with your positive attitude.* Make a point about connecting with as many adults as you can during the day and strive to make those interactions remarkably positive. Compete with yourself daily as to how many co-teachers and staff members you can motivate to smile or laugh. Be contagious with your positive energy! That contagiousness will have a domino effect with students.

Hopefully, this book has given you some actionable items that will help you stave off burnout. We need to proactively look for joy in our profession. We cannot give away what we do not have. Joyful teachers teach happy students. Cultivate realistic optimism and become a warrior against counterproductive attitudes. Do not wear the badge of exhaustion. Know that wherever you are, there is a community *rooting for you!*

References

Alleydog.com (2022). Definition of optimism. Retrieved from: https://www.alleydog.com/glossary/definition.php?term=Optimism.

Appleby, D.C. (2018). Using humor in the college classroom: The pros and cons. Psychology Teacher Network, February 2018 issue. Retrieved from: https://www.apa.org/ed/precollege/ptn/2018/02/humor-college-classroom.

Beazley, C. (2017). 8 Types of Optimism: What are the Dangers of Optimism? Retrieved from: http://positivepsychology.org.uk/the-many-sides-of-optimism/.

BrainyQuote.com (2022). "Begin at the beginning and go on till you come to the end; then stop." Quote attributed to Lewis Carroll. Retrieved from: https://www.brainyquote.com/quotes/lewis_carroll_107140.

Buxman, K. (2015). 30-Day Humor Challenge: Catastrophization (Day 21). YouTube video from: https://www.youtube.com/watch?v=zGaw7jf8cto.

Carver, C. S., Scheier, M. F., & Segerstrom, S. C. (2010). Optimism. *Clinical psychology review*, *30*(7), 879-889. doi: 10.1016/j.cpr.2010.01.006.

Celestine, N. (2019). What Is the Life Orientation Test and How Do We Use It? (LOT-R). Retrieved from: https://positivepsychology.com/life-orientation-test-revised/.

Eatough, E. (2021). How to recover from burnout and love your life again. Retrieved from: https://www.betterup.com/blog/how-to-recover-from-burnout.

Ekman, P. (2021). What is fear? Retrieved from: https://www.paulekman.com/universal-emotions/what-is-fear/.

Hattie, J. (2017). Visible Learning: Backup of Hattie's ranking list of 256 influences and effect sizes related to student achievement. Retrieved from: https://visible-learning.org/backup-hattie-ranking-256-effects-2017/.

Hardy, B. (2020). 8 Science-Backed Ways to Increase your Hope. Retrieved from: https://forge.medium.com/10-science-based-ways-to-increase-your-hope-430892caacb2.

Harvard Health Publishing (2008). Optimism and your health. Retrieved from: https://www.health.harvard.edu/heart-health/optimism-and-your-health.

Heath, C., and D. Heath (2010). Switch: How to change things when change is hard. Danvers, MA 01923: Crown Business Publishing. ISBN-13:978-0385528757.

Heschmat, S. (2018). What is loss aversion? *Psychology Today*. Retrieved from: https://www.psychologytoday.com/us/blog/science-choice/201803/what-is-loss-aversion.

Hodson, G., & MacInnis, C. C. (2016). Derogating humor as a delegitimization strategy in intergroup contexts. *Translational Issues in Psychological Science*, 2(1), 63. Retrieved from: https://www.apa.org/pubs/journals/features/tps-tps0000052.pdf.

Houston, E. (2019). What are attributional and explanatory styles in psychology? Retrieved from: https://positivepsychology.com/explanatory-styles-optimism/.

Lam, L. (n.d.). Your thoughts determine your outcome: Breaking the fear cycle. Retrieved from: https://lisalamcoach.com/2017/03/02/breaking-the-fear-cycle/.

Levin, I. P., Schreiber, J., Lauriola, M., & Gaeth, G. J. (2002). A tale of two pizzas: Building up from a basic product versus scaling down from a fully-loaded product. *Marketing Letters*, 13(4), 335–44.

Martin, R. A., & Lefcourt, H. M. (1984). Situational Humor Response Questionnaire: Quantitative measure of sense of humor. *Journal of personality and social psychology*, 47(1). Retrieved from: https://www.researchgate.net/.

Merriam-Webster (2020). Definition of optimism. Retrieved from: https://www.merriam-webster.com/dictionary/optimism.

Moore, C. (2019). Learned optimism: Is Martin Seligman's glass half full? Retrieved from: https://positivepsychology.com/learned-optimism/#:~:text=Learned%20optimism%20is%20a%20concept,position%20to%20enhance%20our%20wellbeing.

Nortje, A. (2020). Optimistic explanatory styles: Five examples of how to foster it. Retrieved from: https://positivepsychology.com/optimistic-explanatory-style/.

PositivePsychology.com (Ackerman, C., 2018). What is positive psychology? Why is it important? Retrieved from: https://positivepsychology.com/what-is-positive-psychology-definition/#founder-positive-psychology.

Proyer, R. T., Ruch, W., & Buschor, C. (2013). Testing strengths-based interventions: A preliminary study on the effectiveness of a program targeting curiosity, gratitude, hope, humor, and zest for enhancing life satisfaction. *Journal of Happiness Studies, 14*(1), 275–92.

Psychology Today (2022). What is optimism? Retrieved from: https://www.psychologytoday.com/us/basics/optimism.

Psychtests.com (2022). Locus of control and attributional style test. Retrieved from: https://testyourself.psychtests.com/testid/2109.

Rozanski, A., Bavishi, C., Kubzansky, L. D., & Cohen, R. (2019). Association of optimism with cardiovascular events and all-cause mortality: a systematic review and meta-analysis. *JAMA Network Open, 2*(9), e1912200-e1912200.

Scheier, M. F., & Carver, C. S. (2018). Dispositional optimism and physical health: A long look back, a quick look forward. *American Psychologist, 73*(9), 1082.

Scheier, M. F., Carver, C. S., & Bridges, M. W. (1994). Distinguishing optimism from neuroticism (and trait anxiety, self-mastery, and self-esteem): a reevaluation of the Life Orientation Test. *Journal of personality and social psychology, 67*(6), 1063.

Seligman, M. P. (as cited in University of Pennsylvania's Positive Psychology Center, 2022). Attributional Style Questionnaire. Retrieved from: https://ppc.sas.upenn.edu/resources/questionnaires-researchers/attributional-style-questionnaire#:~:text=The%20ASQ%20is%20a%20self,and%20global%20versus%20specific%20causes.

VeryWellMind.com (Scott, 2020). What is optimism? Retrieved from: https://www.verywellmind.com/the-benefits-of-optimism-3144811#:~:text=Optimism%20is%20a%20mental%20attitude,pessimists%20instead%20predict%20unfavorable%20outcomes.

VeryWellMind.com (Cherry, 2020). What is cognitive bias? Retrieved from: https://www.verywellmind.com/what-is-a-cognitive-bias-2794963.

VeryWellMind.com (Cherry, K. (2021). What is emotional detachment? Retrieved from: https://www.verywellmind.com/what-is-emotional-detachment-5121166.

VeryWellMind.com (Cherry, K., 2021). Attitudes and behavior in psychology. Retrieved from: https://www.verywellmind.com/attitudes-how-they-form-change-shape-behavior-2795897.

Willingham, D. T. (2009). Why don't students like school? Because the mind is not designed for thinking. *The American Educator,* Spring 2009. Retrieved from: https://www.aft.org/sites/default/files/periodicals/WILLINGHAM%282%29.pdf.

www.ingramcontent.com/pod-product-compliance
Lightning Source LLC
Chambersburg PA
CBHW021859230426
43671CB00006B/456